WATERSIDE
In The Cots............

Nigel Vile

COUNTRYSIDE BOOKS
NEWBURY, BERKSHIRE

COUNTRYSIDE BOOKS
3 Catherine Road
Newbury, Berkshire

To view our complete range of books,
please visit us at
www.countrysidebooks.co.uk

ISBN 1 85306 604 4

Designed by Graham Whiteman
Cover illustration by Colin Doggett
Maps and photographs by the author

Produced through MRM Associates Ltd., Reading
Typeset by Techniset Typesetters, Newton-le-Willows
Printed by J. W. Arrowsmith Ltd., Bristol

Contents

AREA MAP SHOWING LOCATION OF THE WALKS

Walk

PUBLISHER'S NOTE
We hope that you obtain considerable enjoyment from this book; great care has been taken in its preparation. Although at the time of publication all routes followed public rights of way or permitted paths, diversion orders can be made and permissions withdrawn.

We cannot of course be held responsible for such diversion orders and any inaccuracies in the text which result from these or any other changes to the routes nor any damage which might result from walkers trespassing on private property. We are anxious though that all details covering the walks are kept up to date and would therefore welcome information from readers which would be relevant to future editions.

INTRODUCTION

The sight and sound of water hold a fascination for both young and old alike, with waterborne leisure activities exercising a strong appeal to all age groups. Whether it be youngsters simply paddling in a river, their grandfathers fly fishing on some sparkling stream or their parents yachting on the open seas, there is something alluring about the waterside. Combine a stretch of water with walking, the most popular leisure activity in the country after shopping, and the result is a waterside walk.

The best known of the Cotswold's rivers and streams flow south and east from the high wolds in the north of the region to join the River Thames. Many of the finest Cotswold villages are found in the valleys of these clear-watered streams. The Evenlode rises above Stow-on-the-Wold, before flowing eastwards through Oxfordshire to join the Thames near Eynsham. The Windrush comes south from near Temple Guiting and, after collecting the waters of the Dikler and making Bourton-on-the-Water a miniature Venice with its bridges, it too enters Oxfordshire. At Lechlade come the waters of the Coln by way of Fairford and Bibury, deepening the Thames enough to allow London barges to reach this market town in years gone by.

To allow waterborne traffic to venture further west, a canal system was cut to link the Thames with the Severn. This involved the construction of the Thames and Severn Canal to Chalford, beyond which barges could follow the Stroudwater Canal onto the Severn at Framilode. As well as passing through the aptly named Golden Valley above Stroud, the Thames and Severn Canal also had to carve an impressive course through a 2-mile-long tunnel that pierced the high wolds west of Cirencester. The Romans built this famous town on the banks of the Churn, another of the Thames tributaries, whose source at Seven Springs near Coberley can actually claim to be more distant from the sea than the official source of the Thames at Coates, a mile or two above Kemble.

Many guidebooks appear to give the impression that the Cotswolds extend no further south than Cirencester, but this is patently not the case. The official Cotswold Area of Outstanding Natural Beauty actually stretches as far down as the Avon Valley south of Bath, right to the fringes of Bradford-on-Avon in West Wiltshire. This brings another series of rivers and waterways into the picture, including the River Avon itself which rises in the Southern Cotswolds above Malmesbury, before adding beauty and delight to both Bath and Bristol. The Avon, too, has its own network of tributaries, the most picturesque of which must surely be the By Brook which flows down through Castle Combe, arguably the most photographed village in the country. Just as there was a need for an artificial cut to aid navigation around the upper reaches of the Thames, the same was true further south where the Avon was only ever navigable as far upstream as the Bath area. Hence the coming of the Kennet and Avon Canal.

All of these rivers and canals, together with a series of flooded gravel pits known as the Cotswold Water Park, feature in this collection of waterside walks, where an added attraction is a pub at which to start or finish your journey, or encountered along the way. There is a short description of each of these pubs, together with a flavour of the type of food and drink available. Telephone numbers for each pub have been provided so that you can make precise inquiries about opening hours, food availability and so on. There are also brief details about nearby places of interest to help you plan a whole day out if you wish.

The walks range between 2 and 7 miles in length and can all be easily undertaken by the average person, including family groups. The accompanying sketch maps are intended to guide you to the starting point and provide a simple outline of the route. For your further enjoyment I would recommend that you take an Ordnance Survey map with you – these are particularly useful for identifying the main features or views. The numbers of the relevant Landranger (1:50 000) and Outdoor Leisure or Explorer (1:25 000) sheets are given for each walk.

All of the usual advice should go without saying. When parking, do be careful to respect the daily activities of local people and not block any exits or entrances. Also, the British climate almost demands that walkers carry waterproofs, whilst the proximity of water necessarily means mud. Suitable footwear is therefore essential – and please don't forget to remove muddy boots if patronising the pubs along the way. The actions of a few thoughtless walkers have resulted in a small number of publicans turning against the rambling fraternity. Above all, enjoy these walks that explore what is the most quintessential of English landscapes.

Nigel Vile

WALK 1

THE UPPER WINDRUSH VALLEY
NEAR NAUNTON

Explore the heart of the Upper Windrush Valley, where sweeping hillsides plunge down to the diminutive river itself. This is a quiet corner of the Cotswolds, which is all the better for lying off the main tourist trail.

The lake above Harford Farm

The Windrush is a name that will forever be associated with the Cotswold landscape. Arguably the finest of the area's rivers, it flows from its source at Taddington near Snowshill down to the River Thames a few miles west of Oxford. Along the way, the Windrush adds colour and delight to a number of towns and villages, including Bourton-on-the-Water, Burford and Witney. It may sound something of a cliché, but springtime along the banks of the Windrush, with wild flowers in bloom and new-born lambs skipping in the meadows, must surely rank as the archetypal English scene.

This walk explores the Upper Windrush Valley between Naunton and Bourton-on-the-Water. The river itself is little more than a diminutive stream hereabouts – indeed, only a small section of the route actually follows the riverbank – but the walk as a whole gives a fine overview and insight into this section of the river's course.

From Naunton, quiet lanes are followed across the hilltops to the north of the river. Wide vistas open up across the valley, whilst down below the river flows along through a densely wooded valley bottom. It really is a picture postcard scene. A secluded bridleway drops down to the Windrush itself, before a section of the Windrush Way is followed back towards Naunton. This waymarked trail follows the river as closely as possible as it flows between Winchcombe and Bourton-on-the-Water.

This section of the walk provides the first opportunity to actually explore the riverbank. Conservation is the theme in this quiet corner of the valley, with the local ash and willow trees being professionally pollarded to reduce what would otherwise be vigorous growth of foliage above normal grazing height. Pollarding was originally intended to produce light timber and leafy forage material which could be fed to livestock in times of drought. A little way upstream, alongside Harford Farm, the river has been partially dammed to produce a pair of quite delightful lakes. Both Canada geese and heron are common hereabouts, as well as the rather more ubiquitous moorhen and coot.

The walk returns to Naunton from the hilltop to the south of the village. The view from this vantage point is delightful, with the stone cottages in the valley bottom resembling a model village. Naunton is a long, thin settlement that extends along the floor of the Windrush Valley. With a chapel and a church, a pub and a village store, it has seemingly bucked the trend of diminishing amenities found in so many other villages. Certainly it is a friendly place, with the local residents seemingly only too happy to stop and pass the time of day with visitors. Although just off the route at the western end of the village, the church is well worth seeking out. Most noted for its fine Perpendicular tower decorated with a collection of pinnacles and gargoyles, there is also a rather magnificent 15th-century carved stone pulpit as well as a font dating from the same era.

The village pub is the Black Horse Inn, thought to have originally been a pair of farmworker's cottages back in the 17th century. With its beams, exposed stonework, country kitchen chairs, oak pews and

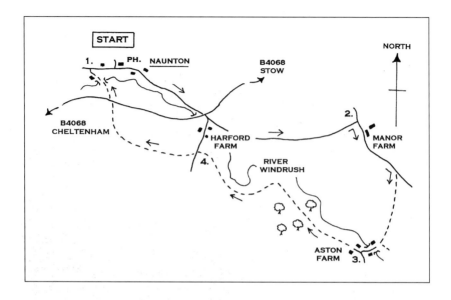

iron-framed tables, it certainly possesses a most traditional feel. Many visitors prefer to relax at one of the tables in front of the Black Horse, with a rather pleasant outlook along Naunton's quiet main street.

A good selection of food is available at the Black Horse, with lesser appetites perhaps favouring home-made soup or sandwiches, whilst heartier appetites might opt for steak and kidney pudding, lasagne or gammon and egg. If fish is your preference, perhaps the bass in a wine and mushroom sauce will prove tempting. Being a Donnington's house, one of their brews such as BB or SBA should be an almost compulsory choice with your meal. Donnington's, based in nearby Stow-on-the-Wold, enjoy a most enviable location and reputation. The brewery is in a 13th-century mill alongside the River Dikler and the various ales have earned good reviews from real ale buffs. The Black Horse's telephone number is 01451 850565.

- **HOW TO GET THERE:** Head for a minor crossroads on the B4068, 4 miles west of Stow-on-the-Wold. At this point, leave the main road and follow an unclassified road northwards, signposted to Naunton. In 1 mile, the road reaches the Black Horse Inn at Naunton.
- **PARKING:** There is room for careful roadside parking on the main street in Naunton in the vicinity of the Black Horse and the village

Naunton, nestled deep in the Windrush Valley

shop. Just above the shop, the road widens and is particularly suited to parking.

- **LENGTH OF THE WALK:** 6 miles. Maps: OS Landranger 163 Cheltenham and Cirencester and OS Outdoor Leisure 45 The Cotswolds (GR 117234).

THE WALK

1. Walk along Naunton's main street, passing the village shop and the Black Horse Inn. Continue along this quiet lane out of Naunton for ³/₄ mile to the B4068. All the while, the infant River Windrush is flowing parallel to the road in the field on the right. Cross the B4068, and follow the lane opposite that climbs steeply uphill, ignoring the right fork to Harford Farm. Follow this lane for 1¹/₄ miles as it crosses the hilltop, fine views across the Windrush Valley on the right. On reaching a road junction, turn right along an occasionally busy unclassified road signposted to Bourton-on-the-Water.

2. In ¹/₂ mile, fork right off the road onto a bridleway. Follow this enclosed track to a gate, before continuing along the bridleway as it

11

runs downhill along the left edges of the next two fields into the valley bottom. In the corner of the second field, pass through a gateway and continue on downhill along an enclosed path to a junction by an isolated stable block. Turn right – signposted 'Windrush Way' – and pass through a small hamlet alongside the Windrush. Cross the river, and follow the lane on uphill to a junction.

3. Turn right, and pass through the complex of buildings that make up Aston Farm. Beyond the last of the barns, follow an uncultivated strip across an arable field towards the woodland opposite. Enter the woodland, and follow the well-worn path through the trees for $1/2$ mile. Leave the woodland at a gate, before following the right-hand edge of a field to a gate in the corner. Beyond this gate, bear left downhill through an area of scrubland to reach the valley bottom and the River Windrush. Follow the river upstream across four fields, heading away from the river in the final field to a gate in the field boundary, just south of Harford Farm.

4. Join a lane, turn left and climb the hillside for 75 yards, before turning right to enter the top of a hillside field, a small lake down below in the valley bottom. Bear left, and walk the whole length of three valley bottom fields, passing through gateways in the end field boundaries along the way. Beyond the gate at the end of the third field, turn right, cross a small clapper bridge and follow the footpath that bears left uphill towards a marker post on the hilltop. Continue beyond this post to a gate at the top of the field. Beyond this gate, continue ahead along a path that crosses the local golf course to reach the B4068. Cross to the gateway opposite, before following the path ahead that leads downhill into the Windrush Valley and Naunton. In 150 yards, where the main path bears sharply left, keep ahead downhill to a gate and the Windrush. Cross the river, and take the lane on the left that climbs up to the main street in Naunton. A right turn will return you to the village shop and the Black Horse Inn.

PLACES OF INTEREST NEARBY
The Cotswold Farm Park, home to rare breed conservation, lies just 3 miles north of Naunton. The Gloucester Old Spot pigs are a particularly appropriate breed at the park. Telephone 01451 850307 for further information.

WALK 2

THE RIVER EVENLODE AT BLEDINGTON

A quiet, almost secretive, walk across the meadows near the picturesque Cotswold village of Bledington. The Evenlode meanders across a broad valley, where the only intrusion is the sound of the occasional train passing between the Midlands and Oxford.

Bledington village green

The River Evenlode has its source in a series of springs high on the wolds between Stow and Moreton. From deep in Gloucestershire, the river flows south, then east through Oxfordshire to join the Glyme, just above its confluence with the Thames east of Eynsham. Bledington lies in the upper reaches of the Evenlode, where the somewhat diminutive river meanders its way across lush water meadows in the heart of what is a broad valley. In midsummer, the river can be little more than a trickle, but in the depths of winter you will be cursing yourself if those walking boots are not well-

13

waxed, with the meadows more akin to primeval marshland. Moisture loving trees and plants, including large numbers of pollarded willows, line the riverbank, which acts as a magnet for traditional British wildfowl. Unfortunately, this is one of those walks where the footpath takes the most direct route, avoiding the twists and turns of the meandering Evenlode. This does mean that walkers who stick rigidly to the right-of-way will only catch occasional glimpses of the river. Meandering footsteps are advisable!

The walk sets off from the quite delightful village of Bledington, where even the most hardened of passing motorists cannot but be impressed by the charming village green, overlooked by any number of highly desirable Cotswold cottages and houses. The village local – the King's Head – looks proudly across the village green, which is dissected by a tributary stream of the Evenlode. A quiet back lane leads from the green to the village church, which is best known for its magnificent Perpendicular windows. The beautiful stained glass is believed to be the work of John Prudde, the well-known Westminster craftsman.

Quiet lanes and fieldpaths bring the walk to the Evenlode and the waterside section of the ramble, before the gentle slopes on the eastern side of the broad valley are followed into the neighbouring village of Kingham. This is yet another exquisite Cotswold village, where we find another village green surrounded by picture postcard cottages and overlooked by the local hostelry. At the opposite end of the village lies the most handsome 17th-century rectory, alongside St Andrew's church. The guidebooks are quick to point out the most unusual, if somewhat stark, stone pew ends in the church, where another highlight is the monument to Lieutenant-Colonel Davis, showing a soldier leaning on his tomb with a reversed rifle. From Kingham, our steps head back across the Evenlode Valley.

The delightful location of the King's Head in Bledington, overlooking the village green and a stream, gives it a head start in the popularity stakes ... but the location is not the only reason why it attracts visitors from far and near. Internally, there is a traditional main bar with old beams, high-backed wooden settles and a wintertime log fire in a stone inglenook. The lounge overlooks the inn's garden, and is furnished with a collection of antiques and paintings. The garden itself is an equally appealing place to linger and enjoy refreshment, sitting as it does alongside that tributary stream of the Evenlode.

The highlight, however, at this charming stone hostelry must be the wide choice of well-prepared food that is available. There are, of course, the normal staples. These include soup, ploughman's, sandwiches and salads. More substantial appetites might be tempted by the specials, that have included such imaginative options as local rabbit wrapped in spinach with a sherry and berry sauce, filo parcels of parma ham and ratatouille on Stilton sauce, steak and mushroom pie and tartlet of mushrooms with watercress dressing. A quite excellent selection of beers is also available, which could typically include brews from Adnams, Hook Norton and Wadworth. Being in the Cotswolds, however, the natural choice should be Uley Old Spot, named after a well-known breed of Gloucestershire pigs! Telephone: 01608 658365.

- **HOW TO GET THERE:** Bledington lies 5 miles south-east of Stow-on-the-Wold, on the B4450 road to Chipping Norton.
- **PARKING:** Entering Bledington from Stow-on-the-Wold direction, take the second turning on the right that runs across the southern edge of the village green. Park carefully on the roadside alongside the green, just across the way from the King's Head.
- **LENGTH OF THE WALK:** 4 miles. Maps: OS Landranger 163 Cheltenham and Cirencester and OS Outdoor Leisure 45 The Cotswolds (GR 243228).

THE WALK

1. Walk back down to the B4450 and on into the centre of Bledington. Where the main road bears right by the post office, keep ahead along Chapel Lane, a cul-de-sac. Continue along this lane for 250 yards until it bears right and ends up at a cottage. Continue along the track to the right of this cottage, which leads around to a gateway and an open field. Cross the stile by this gate, turn left and head down to a footbridge in the end field boundary. Cross a small stream before heading across the next field to a stile and the trackbed of the former branch line to Bourton-on-the-Water. Cross the trackbed and follow the footpath to the right as it runs alongside a hedgerow. Where this hedgerow bears sharply to the left, continue ahead across the field towards the bridge opposite that crosses the Evenlode. Just before reaching this bridge, cross a stile by a gate on the left into a riverside meadow.

15

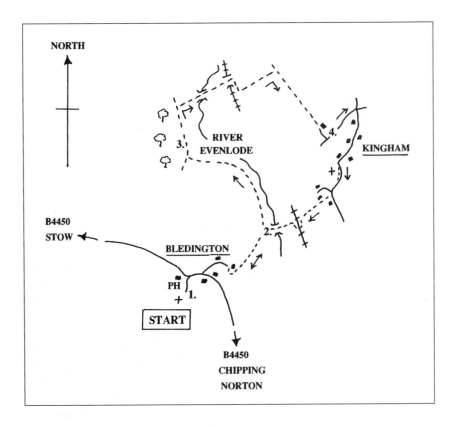

2. Head across to a gate on the far side of this field, the river itself meandering away on the right-hand side. Cross a stile alongside this gate into a second riverside pasture, where we temporarily leave the river which passes behind the main Midlands to Oxford railway line on the right. We continue along the footpath, which follows the left edge of the field around to a gate in the left-hand corner where we rejoin the river. Pass through this gateway, bear right and continue ahead to a belt of trees on the right. Continue ahead, passing to the right of a pond, across to another stile alongside the Evenlode. Follow the right edge of the next field to a stile on the far side, before crossing the next field to reach a stile beneath a large tree. Cross this stile, and continue ahead for a few yards to join a prominent track.

3. Turn right and, in 400 yards, pass through a handgate which is almost hidden in the hedgerow on the right. Cross the field ahead to a footbridge across the Evenlode, cross the river and turn left. Walk across the field to a gateway in the left-hand corner, the Evenlode now on the left. Beyond this gateway, continue uphill to a bridge over the main railway line. Enter the next field, turn right to the corner before turning left to follow the end field boundary up to a prominent track. Turn right, and follow this track for ½ mile into Kingham.

4. Enter the village, and follow a lane down to a tree on a small green and a road junction. Turn left, and follow West Street for 300 yards up to a road junction by the village green. Turn right, and follow the main road through the village for 600 yards down to the church. Immediately past the church, pass through a kissing gate on the right to follow a tarmac path across the enclosure below the church. Rejoin the main road, turn right and continue ahead to the junction of Station Road with New Road. Keep ahead at this point along the grassy path signposted to Bledington. On reaching a gate, follow this path to the left for 20 yards to another gate, this time on the right-hand side. Cross the main railway, before bearing right to another gateway. Bear half-left across the next field, walking diagonally to reach a wooden footbridge that crosses a normally dry stream. Then continue ahead to reach that footbridge across the Evenlode passed at the outset. It is now a simple question of retracing your steps back into Bledington. Having crossed the river, cross the field to the corner of the hedgerow opposite before following the hedge on the right back to the old railway trackbed. Cross the trackbed to a stile opposite, head across the next field to a footbridge over a tributary of the Evenlode before making for a gate in the top right corner of the next field. Follow the track beyond this gate back into Chapel Lane which is then followed back to the B4450.

PLACES OF INTEREST NEARBY
The Toy and Collector's Museum in nearby Stow-on-the-Wold presents a fascinating collection of teddy bears, dolls, trains and games. Telephone 01451 830159 for further details.

THE RIVER WINDRUSH AT BOURTON-ON-THE-WATER

Bourton-on-the-Water, with its series of ornamental bridges spanning the clear waters of the Windrush, has earned a reputation as being 'the Venice of the Cotswolds'. A slight exaggeration, of course, but this is undoubtedly 'an unashamedly pretty place' to quote one local guidebook. This delightful walk from Bourton includes the River Dikler as well as the Quarry Lakes.

Visitors to Bourton-on-the-Water inevitably sense a feeling of déja vu. Those diminutive footbridges across the Windrush, the broad tree-lined greens bordering the riverbank and the delightful Cotswold architecture have graced calendars, chocolate boxes and greetings cards up and down the country. This is without a shadow of doubt a real tourist mecca, one of the Cotswold's honeypots, so be sure to arrive early, enjoy looking around the village before the coach parties arrive and then set off on what is a thoroughly enjoyable waterside walk in the heart of Gloucestershire.

Along the way, the walk borders both the Windrush and the lesser-known River Dikler, a tributary stream that flows down from Stow-on-the-Wold. Also less well-known are the 'Quarry Lakes', a series of flooded gravel workings on which a number of nature reserves are being established. Swans, moorhens, mallards and Canada geese are common hereabouts, together with many seasonal visitors that include the occasional common sandpiper, sand martins, reed buntings and redpolls. The lakes are also popular with fishermen, with the lake passed at the outset being stocked with trout, and the lakes passed at journey's end being heavily used for coarse fishing, with carp and pike being particularly common.

Away from Bourton's waterside, the walk climbs a neighbouring hillside to visit Little Rissington, whose attractive cottages and houses lie to the south of the village church, which enjoys a solitary location on the very edge of the hilltop. Aside from the Norman south doorway, the church is largely a 19th-century restoration which singularly fails to excite the imagination of any guidebook writer. St Peter's is most often visited by relatives of pilots killed during the last war, who were based on a nearby airfield which housed the RAF's Central Flying School. The lines of white gravestones in the churchyard are indeed a poignant reminder of the debt we owe to a former generation of young men.

Just before journey's end in Bourton-on-the-Water, the walk passes the oddly named Old New Inn. This unchanging old hotel bears an interesting sign on its frontage which declares 'Old Inn 1712 New Inn 1938', a clue as to the history of this comfortably worn and welcoming inn. It sits alongside a 1:9 scale model of the village, which was created in the 1930s by the landlord's father. The inn's back bar, with its big painted panels and collection of beer bottles, is particularly interesting.

An extensive menu awaits visitors to the Old New Inn. At the lighter end of the market, ploughman's, sandwiches and soups are available, whilst heartier appetites might prefer to tuck into grilled trout with almonds, roast leg of lamb or Gloucester sausages, all served with a good array of trimmings. In between are such tempting options as roll mop herring salad, smoked mackerel and lentil and mushroom bake. The Old New Inn offers particularly well-kept Bass, as well as regular guest beers. Telephone: 01451 820467.

- **HOW TO GET THERE:** Bourton-on-the-Water lies just off of the A429 road running between Cirencester and Stow-on-the-Wold. Four miles south of Stow, prominent signs direct visitors from the main road into the village.
- **PARKING:** Follow the signs in Bourton-on-the-Water to the local Birdland attraction. Alongside the entrance to Birdland is a public car park. Payment for 4 hour's parking time should be sufficient to complete the walk and enjoy a bite to eat.
- **LENGTH OF THE WALK:** 4 miles. Maps: OS Landranger 163 Cheltenham and Cirencester and OS Outdoor Leisure 45 The Cotswolds (GR 169204).

THE WALK

1. Leave the car park, turn right and follow the Little Rissington road out of Bourton-on-the-Water. In 400 yards, turn right into Hilcote Drive. Almost immediately, keep left where the road forks. In just a few yards, just past a property called Rosewarne, turn right down an enclosed footpath which runs between the back gardens of two neighbouring properties down to a stile. Continue along another section of enclosed footpath before entering an open field, with the River Windrush over on the right-hand side. Walk down the right edge of this field to a stile in the corner, pass through a short section of woodland – crossing the Windrush – to a stile, before turning left to follow the left edge of a field running alongside the river. In the corner of this field, cross a pair of stiles to reach a junction of paths. Keep directly ahead, following a path that runs through the trees that lie alongside the Windrush. Continue along this enclosed path for 250 yards to a squeezebelly stile, and turn left along the edge of a field towards a gate and a barn. Just before this gate, cross a stile on the left and a bridge over the Windrush, to reach the banks of a lake.

2. Follow the edge of the lake to the right – it is soon followed by a second smaller lake. Where the water ends, bear left to follow the southern end of the lake. Cross to the far side of the lakeside enclosure to reach a handgate, and continue along an enclosed path that runs through to a footbridge over the River Dikler. Cross this bridge, and bear left to follow an enclosed path up to a lane. Turn left and, in 100 yards, just past a barn in the field on the left, cross a gate on the right to follow a signposted footpath. Head uphill across

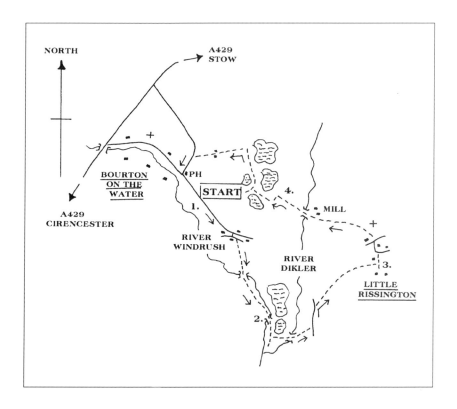

the middle of the first field towards the top left corner, fine views opening up behind across the lakes passed earlier. In the top corner of the field, pass through a gateway into the next field. Bear right, clipping the corner of the field, to another gateway. In the next field, bear half left, clipping the field corner, to a stile beneath a prominent tree. In the next field, bear half left, clipping the top corner of the field to reach a wooden barrier. Enter a paddock, and cross to a pair of gates in the far left-hand corner. Cross these gates, and walk diagonally to the far right corner of the next field to reach a stile behind a small stable block. Cross this stile and head up the left edge of the next field to reach an unmetalled lane on the edge of Little Rissington.

3. Turn left to a road junction, and keep directly ahead through the village of Little Rissington. At the next junction, follow the footpath opposite signposted to St Peter's church. Pass to the left of the church to reach a wooden gate, and continue into the adjoining field. Head directly across this field in the direction of Bourton-on-the-Water to a stile, before dropping downhill in the next field, bearing half-right to reach a stile halfway down the right-hand field boundary. In the next field, head directly across to the opposite corner to reach a gate/stile and a quiet lane. Follow the lane ahead down towards Rissington Mill. Where the lane bears right to the mill, cross a stile ahead between a pair of conifers, and walk down the right edge of a field, Rissington Mill to the right. Pass through a gate in the corner of this field, and continue directly ahead between a tennis court and the mill. Cross the millstream and the River Dikler before entering a meadow. Bear right, following the Dikler on the right. Shortly, cross a stile in the hedge over on the left, and head directly across the next field to a wooden gate opposite.

4. Beyond this gate, cross a small footbridge over a ditch before continuing along a path that bears left to follow the edge of a lake. Follow this path all of the way around the south-western edge of the lake until you reach a junction amidst a group of lakes. Turn right along an unmetalled track until you come to three gates. Pass through the middle gateway and follow the left edge of the lake ahead. In the far left corner of this enclosure, cross a stile on the left and walk through an area of scrub to reach a second stile. Cross this stile, and another stile immediately ahead, before continuing directly ahead along a grassy path that leads to the complex of farm buildings 200 yards ahead that make up Salmonsbury Farm. Follow the path between the farm buildings, crossing a couple of gates, before continuing down the drive away from the farm down to the main road leading into Bourton-on-the-Water. Turn left and, in 200 yards, a junction presents you with two possibilities. A right turn brings you into the centre of Bourton-on-the-Water, whilst a left turn takes you past the Old New Inn back to the Birdland car park.

PLACES OF INTEREST NEARBY

Bourton-on-the-Water has a range of tourist attractions that include *Birdland*, the *Model Village*, the *Cotswold Motor Museum & Village Life Exhibition* and the *Model Railway*. Birdland, established by the late Len Hill, lies in a streamside garden, and includes a lively display of penguins. Telephone Stow-on-the-Wold Tourist Information Centre on 01451 831082 for further details.

WALK 4

THE RIVER WINDRUSH
DOWNSTREAM OF BURFORD

Leave behind the hustle and bustle of Burford's High Street and head out for the lush water meadows that border the Windrush as it flows downstream to Swinbrook. The delightful Swan Inn alongside the river at Swinbrook makes a perfect resting spot along the way.

Arthur Mee's guidebook to Gloucestershire was rather perfunctory about the Windrush. In this volume of *The King's England*, Arthur Mee noted that 'the Windrush comes south from near Temple Guiting and, after collecting the waters of the Dickler and making Bourton-on-the-Water a miniature Venice with its bridges, enters Oxfordshire.' At Burford, of course, the Windrush has entered Oxfordshire and is well on course for its confluence with the Thames downstream of Witney.

On this walk, our steps follow the Windrush Valley downstream from Burford, through Widford and Swinbrook almost as far as Asthall. The water meadows below Burford are an absolute delight, especially when expectant sheep are grazing in the riverside pastures. With swans, moorhens, coot and ducks making their home along the riverbank, it is a quintessentially English scene.

Widford is a fascinating hamlet. There is the obligatory mill on the river, but of rather more interest is St Oswald's church standing in splendid isolation in the middle of the meadows. The medieval village of Widford lay to the west of the church, but was abandoned at the time of the Black Death, leaving the solitary church building as a reminder of former times. The interior is delightfully unspoilt, with its box pews and 14th-century wall paintings. The church was built on the site of a Roman villa but, unfortunately, fragments of a mosaic floor have been removed from public viewing due to the actions of a few thoughtless visitors.

Lovers of church architecture will find much of interest at the church in neighbouring Swinbrook. There is the unusual tower and the fine Perpendicular east window, as well as the gravestone of Unity Mitford outside in the churchyard. It is the Fettiplace monuments, however, that will surely catch the eye. Swinbrook was the home of this now extinct family, with their mansion lying below the church and above the Windrush. The monuments consist of two fascinating trios of reclining gentlemen, one group Tudor, the other Stuart. All six gentlemen are reclining on their right sides, and defy convention by looking outwards rather than upwards! The clear glass of the east window means that the monuments are flooded with light, which only adds to their dramatic impact.

From the church, the walk descends to the Swan Inn at Swinbrook, before climbing onto the hilltop above the village. From here, good views open up across the Windrush Valley and this secluded corner of Oxfordshire. From the hilltops, a gentle descent brings the walk back to St Oswald's church in Widford, from where we retrace our steps along the Windrush back into Burford. Although this is familiar ground, walking upstream rather than downstream places an entirely different perspective on this watery landscape.

Burford itself is a delightfully picturesque spot. Its wide main street descends steeply from the high wolds to the Windrush Valley, with the whole scene admirably overlooked by the parish church. There is a Norman tower capped by a slender 15th-century spire, dating from the time when Burford's prosperity from the wool trade was at its peak. The town is understandably popular with visitors, and its busy High Street contrasts vividly with the tranquil riverside walk downstream to Widford and Swinbrook.

As this is one of the longer walks the Swan Inn at Swinbrook, formerly the village mill, comes at a convenient point along the way. The stone-built 400-year-old pub, with its splendid wisteria climbing all over the front walls, really is an unspoilt village inn. With its flagstone flooring, beams, simple antique furnishings and wood-burning stove, it exudes a most traditional atmosphere. Old fashioned wooden benches at the front of the inn provide an excellent spot to linger and restore those flagging limbs on a warm day.

The choice of dishes ranges from sandwiches through to more substantial offerings such as home-made steak and kidney pie, fish pie and seafood platter. There is also a carpeted restaurant, which offers some excellent fish and game dishes, although this is probably not the place for mud-splattered walkers to wine and dine. Good beers available at the Swan include Morland Original and Wadworth 6X, traditional brews to accompany fine food in a good old English pub. Telephone: 01993 822165.

- **HOW TO GET THERE/PARKING:** Burford lies just north of the A40, midway between Oxford and Cheltenham. Leave the A40 just to the south of the town and follow the A361 into the town centre. At the bottom of the High Street, follow the signs to the free car park which lies at the end of Church Lane.
- **HOW TO GET THERE:** 7 miles. Maps: OS Landranger 163 Cheltenham and Cirencester and OS Outdoor Leisure 45 The Cotswolds (GR 255123).

THE WALK

1. Leave the car park, cross the footbridge over the Windrush and turn left to follow a side street up to the road junction by the Royal Oak Inn. Turn left, and follow an unclassified road out of Burford for ½ mile, before turning left onto a footpath signposted to Widford. This path enters the meadows beside the Windrush. Follow the river downstream across four fields. At the far side of the final field, bear right away from the river up to a gate and a quiet lane.

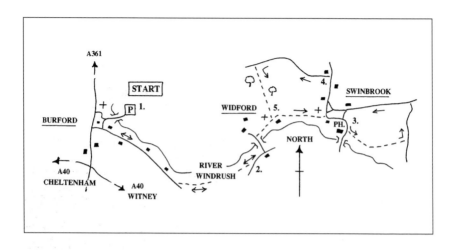

2. Turn left and, in 100 yards, left again down the cul-de-sac lane by Widford Mill Farm. Cross a millstream and the Windrush before passing a small lake in the field on the right. Immediately past this lake, turn right by a cattle grid to follow the footpath signposted to Swinbrook. Cross the first field to a gateway, where an obligatory detour to the left will enable you to visit St Oswald's church. In the next field, keep directly ahead to the gateway opposite, passing a cottage on the right-hand side. In the following field, head across to a gate opposite, before continuing along an enclosed path to the main street in Swinbrook, passing to the right of the church along the way. Turn right, and follow the lane down through the village to the Swan Inn, just before the bridge across the Windrush.

3. Just before the Swan, cross a stone slab stile on the left and head across a field, following the path signposted to Asthall. Pass through the gateway opposite, and in the next field follow the left-hand field boundary to a gate in the far left corner. Follow the left edge of the next field to a stile in the corner and a country lane. Turn left, follow this lane uphill for 300 yards to a junction and turn left to follow the road signposted to Swinbrook. This quiet byway brings good views on the left-hand side across the Windrush Valley. On reaching Swinbrook, keep right at the junction just past the speed restriction signs, right again at the junction by Stocks Cottage and then right once more at the next junction to follow the main street north out of Swinbrook as far as a junction by The Forge.

Widford church

4. Turn left and follow this lane for ½ mile, initially climbing steeply uphill. Where the lane drops downhill into a dip, turn left to follow the footpath signposted to Widford. Follow this path down through Dean Bottom, a linear field bordered by woodland. At the foot of the field, cross a stile to enter a meadow below St Oswald's church. Head across to a gate on the right to rejoin the path followed at the outset.

5. Retrace your steps to Burford, reversing the outward leg of the walk. This brings a different perspective to the landscape, especially walking along the riverside section of the walk. On reaching the Royal Oak, continue ahead to Burford's High Street. Turn right, and follow the High Street down as far as Church Lane, where a right turn takes you past the church and back to the car park.

PLACES OF INTEREST NEARBY
Burford can boast the *Cotswold Wildlife Park*, with a variety of wild creatures that range from leaf-cutting ants to rare Asiatic lions (telephone: 01993 823006), as well as *Glass Heritage*, home to a glass studio that will both design and make window or door panels to order (telephone: 01993 822290).

WALK 5

THE RIVER COLN NEAR CHEDWORTH

The rolling hills and secluded valleys around Chedworth provide some of the most idyllic scenery in the Cotswolds. It is not difficult to see why the Romans chose to locate one of their finest villas in this quiet corner of Gloucestershire.

The River Coln

From its source in the hills east of Cheltenham, to its confluence with the Thames just above Lechlade, the River Coln adds beauty and charm to no fewer than 23 villages along its course. Below the Roman villa at Chedworth, the Coln is very much in its infancy, pursuing an often hidden and reclusive path through the sweeping countryside. The walk, despite a rather short riverside section, does present a charming picture of the Upper Coln Valley, with woodland clinging to the sweeping hillsides that border the river's edge.

From the Roman villa, whose pavements, bath house and other

remains are now an important National Trust property, the walk climbs through Chedworth Woods to the neighbouring valley and the village of Chedworth itself. Several springs around the village feed a tributary stream of the Coln, including one impressive spring that bubbles out of the wall opposite the Seven Tuns, the village hostelry. Above the inn stands the late Norman church, overlooking a village whose cottages and lanes lie scattered across steep hillsides. From Chedworth, the walk passes through another quiet corner of Chedworth Woods before following the infant River Coln back to the Roman villa.

Along the way, the Seven Tuns in Chedworth will surely prove an irresistible attraction. Tuns are, of course, brewers' fermenting vats, which give a clue as to the origins of the inn. Beams, stone fireplaces, prints, tankards and historic photographs of the village lend the Seven Tuns a traditional, relaxed feel in which to enjoy a good selection of snacks, meals and drinks.

The standard bar menu includes sandwiches, ploughman's, soup, pâté, beef and ale pie and steaks, whilst the daily specials have included Gloucester Old Spot sausages, fresh Scottish salmon, roast fillet of pork and stir-fried purple sprouting broccoli in garlic butter. To accompany your meal, the beers available include Ruddles County, Courage Directors and Georges Traditional. The raised terrace garden across the road from the Seven Tuns is a quite excellent spot to linger with some fine food and drink, with the return leg of the walk guaranteed to help you walk off any excess calories consumed along the way. Telephone: 01285 720242.

- **HOW TO GET THERE:** Turn off the A429 8 miles north of Cirencester, at Fossebridge, and follow the unclassified road signposted to Chedworth Roman Villa. The villa lies 3 miles from the A429, and is signposted at all subsequent junctions. NB: Do not follow the signs for Chedworth village, which lies in a neighbouring valley.
- **PARKING:** A cul-de-sac lane leads to the Roman villa, outside which parking is reserved for visitors to the villa. Below the villa is a woodland parking area, which walkers should use.
- **LENGTH OF THE WALK:** 4 miles. Maps: OS Landranger 163 Cheltenham and Cirencester and OS Outdoor Leisure 45 The Cotswolds (GR 055134).

THE WALK

1. Leave the woodland parking area and walk back down to the lane, before turning left up to the entrance to Chedworth Roman Villa. Follow the footpath that runs to the left of the entrance building into Chedworth Woods. In 100 yards, the path passes beneath an old railway bridge that once carried trains running between Cirencester and Cheltenham. In another 100 yards, at a crossroads, turn left to follow a path due south through Chedworth Woods, ignoring any side turns along the way. Continue to a stile on the edge of the woodland, enter an open field and head directly uphill towards the fence on the skyline. Continue walking in the same direction, with the fence on your left, to the top left corner of the field. It is worth pausing for breath to enjoy the views back across the Coln Valley.

2. In the corner of the field, ignore the paths that go off on the left, continuing ahead through a metal gate to a stone slab stile and steps that descend the hillside. At the foot of these steps, enter an open field. Head directly across this field until a cottage comes into view on the right. Cross the stile alongside this cottage, before continuing along the lane to Chedworth church. Just past the church, turn sharp left to follow the lane down past the Seven Tuns. Continue through the village, and keep on the road as it climbs steeply out of Chedworth.

3. Where the lane bears sharply to the right halfway up the hill, turn left along the driveway leading to Hartshill. At the entrance to this drive, pass through a handgate on the right to follow a wall/fence uphill, with a fine view of Chedworth in the valley below. In the far corner of this hillside field, pass through a metal gate to reach a junction of paths. Follow the enclosed path on the right for 650 yards until it reaches an open arable field. Head directly across the middle of this hilltop field, following an uncultivated strip, with open views on all sides. At the far side of the field, cross a stile and a track before entering a second arable field. Continue in the same direction across this field to reach a small clump of trees just before the far side of the field. Turn left on reaching this clump, and follow the fieldpath signposted down to Chedworth Woods.

4. Enter the woods, and follow the main woodland track for 500

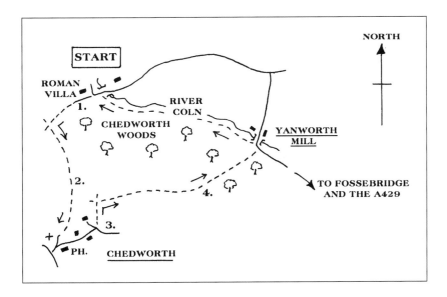

yards, before forking left to follow an arrowed side path. This path soon joins another woodland track, which is followed for just a few yards to another arrowed left turn. Follow this path for 250 yards down to a stile and a quiet lane just above the River Coln near Yanworth Mill. Turn left and, in 25 yards, where the road bears right to cross the Coln, keep ahead along the 'Private Road – Footpath Only'. Follow this unmetalled road for 1¹/₂ miles through to the lane below Chedworth Villa. At first, the Coln is hidden in the bushes on the far side of the meadow on the right, but eventually the track borders the river itself. There are several points where direct access to the river can be obtained. On reaching the green gates and the lane below the villa, turn left and follow the cul-de-sac lane signposted to Chedworth Roman Villa. In 100 yards, turn left along the track leading to the woodland parking area.

PLACES OF INTEREST NEARBY
No visitor to this corner of the Cotswolds should miss *Chedworth Roman Villa* (NT). There are substantial remains of a Romano-British villa, with the pavements and bath house being particularly well-preserved. Telephone: 01242 890256.

WALK 6
THE RIVER CHURN AT NORTH CERNEY

North of Cirencester, the River Churn meanders its way through an archetypal Cotswold landscape. Water meadows lie at the foot of wooded slopes, with churches, cottages and farms fashioned out of the golden local stone lying at every turn.

The Churn Valley

The River Churn flows from its source at Seven Springs, just 3 miles south of Cheltenham, through to the River Thames at Cricklade. It is a delightful watercourse, especially above Cirencester, where the river winds its way in reedy loops through lush meadows that lie below tumbling hillsides. In springtime, with sheep and lambs grazing alongside the river, it really is a picture postcard scene, that would leave any expatriate Englishman feeling faintly nostalgic. The river is also an angler's paradise, whose clear waters are home to trout, perch, dace and a whole host of other coarse fish.

An element of controversy surrounds the Churn. Purists argue that the source of a river is the furthest and highest point of the river from its mouth. If this is the case, then the aforementioned Seven Springs can rightly lay claim to be the source of the Thames ... which would mean the Churn is actually the Thames! That muddy little pool south of Cheltenham, which is quite literally fed by seven springs, has a lot to answer for. It took a parliamentary debate to decide whether Seven Springs or Thames Head, near Kemble, was the official source of the Thames. Our parliamentary representatives opted for Thames Head, which appears as the official source on the OS sheets, but the locals around Seven Springs still dispute this official judgement.

The walk itself begins at North Cerney, a thriving village that can still boast a school, a pub and a church, amenities that have slowly been dwindling in many of our smaller communities. The largely Norman church is best known for its delightful saddleback tower, although the fine south doorway and the 18th-century monument to William Tyndale in the Lady Chapel should not be overlooked. Opposite the church lies the 17th-century rectory, beyond which is the rather handsome Cerney House.

A stiff climb uphill along Chapel Lane brings the walk to Conigree Wood, where a delightful woodland path brings us down to the banks of the Churn itself. The river is followed downstream for 2 miles to the hamlet of Perrott's Brook, where we follow a side valley of the Churn through to Bagendon. Here everything is stone, that delightful golden limestone that so typifies Cotswold towns and villages. A diminutive church, again characterised by a Norman saddleback tower, is the centre of village life. Interestingly, the chancel has been constructed at a higher level than the nave. This oddity dates back to medieval times, with the aim of the construction being to avoid flooding – the local valley is the site of several springs that feed a tributary stream of the Churn. The springs might explain why this is an area of ancient settlement. To the south and west of the village lie Bagendon dykes, the remains of the Iron Age capital of Dobunni.

Back in North Cerney, the walk ends up, as it began, at the Bathurst Arms. Earl Bathurst is a great landowner in this area, with the ancestral home being $3^1/_2$ miles to the south in Cirencester Park. Quite rightly, the inn sign depicts the family coat of arms. This pink-washed and stone-tiled building houses an inn that exudes a most traditional feel. Beams, wood-panelling and open fireplaces are what one would expect in such a hostelry, which is comfortably furnished with old tables, window seats, country chairs and high-backed settles.

The Bathurst Arms' menu, consisting of sandwiches, home-made pâté and salads, through to pasta dishes, home-made pies and daily specials, will give you plenty of choice. The specials might include duck with a sweet and sour sauce or salmon fishcakes. Ostrich with hunter sauce has even been known to make an appearance! To accompany your meal, fine real ales from the West Country brewers such as Arkell's, Hook Norton or Wadworth are usually available. If the weather is fine, there are picnic tables on the lawn in front of the inn, overlooking the river. Telephone: 01285 831281.

- **HOW TO GET THERE:** North Cerney lies 3½ miles north of Cirencester on the A435 road leading to Cheltenham. On entering the village, turn right just past the Bathurst Arms to reach the main part of North Cerney.
- **PARKING:** There is room for roadside parking in North Cerney alongside the Bathurst Arms.
- **LENGTH OF THE WALK:** 6 miles. Maps: OS Landranger 163 Cheltenham and Cirencester and OS Outdoor Leisure 45 The Cotswolds. (GR 019079).

The Walk

1. Continue up the lane alongside the Bathurst Arms. At the junction by a small green, keep left and follow the lane by North Cerney School. Keep on this lane as it climbs uphill, keeping left at one early junction to follow the lane signposted to Withington. This is Chapel Lane, which climbs and winds its way out of North Cerney. In ½ mile, on reaching a hilltop junction, turn left along the road signposted to Withington and Andoversford. In 200 yards, pass through a handgate on the left to follow a signposted bridleway. Cross to the far-right corner of this field, pass through a handgate and join a track. Turn left for a few yards until you reach a handgate on the left. Pass through this gate into Conigree Wood.

2. Follow the main woodland path along the edge of the wood for just under ½ mile to a point where the main path swings right to drop downhill. At this point, fork left to follow a signposted footpath

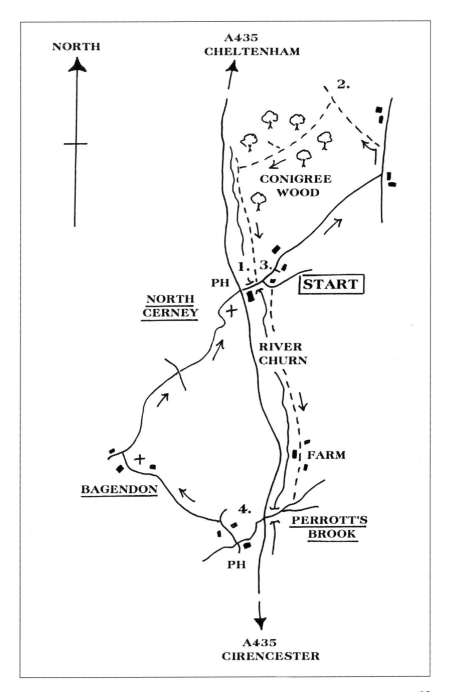

down the edge of the woodland – this is actually the Monarch's Way. At the foot of the slope, by the Churn, pass through a gate on the left to join the riverbank. Follow the river to the far side of the field, and pass through a handgate into a second meadow. Towards the far side of this field, pass through a gate in the wall on the left. Bear right, and follow the fieldpath as it climbs the hillside above – but parallel to – the Churn. Continue along this path to a handgate, before continuing along a track down to the lane in North Cerney.

3. Turn left to return to the green and junction passed earlier, only this time bearing right to follow the lane up and out of the village. A little way up the hill, turn right to follow a signposted bridleway through a gateway into a paddock. In 30 yards, pass through a handgate on the left, turn right and follow the right edges of the next four fields, all the while walking parallel to the Churn which meanders through the meadow on the right. In the corner of the fourth field, beyond a gateway, follow a farm track – which becomes a metalled lane – past the cottages and buildings that make up Perrott's Brook Farm. At the road junction beyond this farm, turn right into Perrott's Brook, before turning right at the next junction to cross the Churn and reach the A435.

4. Cross the A435 and follow the lane opposite, signposted to Daglingworth, passing to the right of the Bear Inn. Shortly, at a crossroads, turn right along the lane signposted to Bagendon. In 200 yards, turn left along the lane leading into Bagendon, following a tributary valley of the Churn. In Bagendon, walk past the church and continue on to the war memorial. Turn right along the lane signposted to North Cerney. In 1/2 mile, at a hilltop crossroads, continue straight over, following the lane, still signposted to North Cerney. Follow this lane on downhill to pass North Cerney church before reaching the A435. Cross over to return to the lane running alongside the Bathurst Arms.

PLACES OF INTEREST NEARBY
If time permits, head south to Cirencester and explore *Cirencester Park*, the ancestral home of Earl Bathurst. The grounds are private, but signs proclaim that 'You are welcome on foot and horseback by permission of the Earl Bathurst'. The park lies immediately west of the town centre.

THE RIVER COLN AT BIBURY

Although just a few miles downstream from the walk at Chedworth, the Coln's appearance at Bibury is altogether different. Fish-bearing, the river glides gently by lawn and meadow on its course towards the Thames at Lechlade.

William Morris, in one of those moments that the local residents have surely regretted for generations, described Bibury as 'the most beautiful village in the Cotswolds'. In a region that can boast so many attractive villages, such praise can but attract excessive numbers of tourists. Few, however, are likely to leave Bibury disappointed.

The village owes much to the presence of the River Coln, which formed the basis of the local woollen trade in centuries past. The much admired Arlington Row was formerly a rank of weavers' cottages, that fronted onto Rack Isle, where local Cotswold wool was spread onto racks to dry. Both properties are now in the care of the

National Trust, although the cottages that form Arlington Row are private residences not open to the public.

Just upstream from Arlington Row is Arlington Mill, a former corn mill whose grindstones and mill machinery now form part of a delightful museum. The economic importance of the Coln continues to this day, with Bibury Trout Farm being yet another of the village attractions. The phrase 'catch your own' takes on a whole new meaning!

From Bibury, the walk follows the Coln Valley downstream to the neighbouring village of Coln St Aldwyn, with several pleasant riverside stretches along the way. The Old Mill stands at the entrance to the village, where a much restored church and an Elizabethan manor house look out over the clear waters of the Coln to the beech woods beyond.

The riverside section of the walk is retraced back to Bibury, where the return to the centre of the village passes Bibury Mill, Bibury Court and a village church whose elegance owes much to the wealth created by the local woollen trade. The attractive 17th and 18th-century cottages and houses throughout the village, clad in climbing roses and honeysuckle in summertime, will certainly have many visitors breaking that commandment about not coveting thy neighbour's house. Perhaps a visit to the church for confessional will be in order!

Conveniently located halfway around the walk is the New Inn at Coln St Aldwyn. This is a wholly appropriate spot to rest and linger awhile whilst enjoying some welcome refreshment. This Cotswold stone hostelry fronts onto the village street, which makes the adjoining terraced garden a particularly enticing spot to sit and enjoy the attractive outlook across the village.

The New Inn, with its low beams and stripped stonework, presents a most traditional feel to visitors. This atmosphere is further enhanced by quarry stone tiles, bunches of hops, a stone fireplace and willow pattern plates. It is a most delightful place to enjoy fine food, that ranges from soup and pâté through to confit of duck, crab and coriander cakes and fillet of brill. Rich chocolate tart and steamed marmalade sponge pudding are but two of the highly calorific puddings available. Accompany your meal with a glass of Hook Norton Best, Wadworth 6X or Morland Original, and you will have all the ingredients that make for a perfect repast. Telephone: 01285 750651.

- **HOW TO GET THERE:** Bibury lies 7 miles north-east of Cirencester on the B4425 road to Burford. This road was formerly the A433, and still appears as such on many road maps.
- **PARKING:** There is free roadside parking in Bibury on the B4425 alongside the River Coln.
- **LENGTH OF THE WALK:** 6 miles. Maps: OS Landranger 163 Cheltenham and Cirencester and OS Outdoor Leisure 45 The Cotswolds (GR 115068).

THE WALK

1. Continue along the pavement beside the Coln to a footbridge, cross the river and walk up past Arlington Row. Beyond this famous rank of weavers' cottages, continue along the lane uphill between a number of attractive properties. On reaching a triangular green at the top of the hill, bear left along a private lane – public footpath – which very soon reaches a metal handgate. Continue along a short section of enclosed path to a wooden gate and a junction of several paths. Continue directly ahead along a track, keeping a wall to your right. At the far side of the field, pass through a gap in the field boundary and turn immediately to the left, to follow the left edge of a field bounded by a wall.

2. On reaching the far side of this field, continue along what becomes an enclosed path for 200 yards before entering another field. Continue along the left edge of this field to the corner, where the route continues along an enclosed track, all the while walking in the same south-easterly direction. In 200 yards, at a junction, turn right. (NB: Having retraced the riverside section of the walk on the return leg, the walk continues from this junction.) Continue along this track for almost ½ mile, walking alongside Oxhill Wood, ignoring a prominent right turn along the way. Eventually, the track drops downhill to reach a stone slab stile and an open field.

3. Head across this field to a gate opposite, where Ash Copse drops down to the Coln. Continue along a short enclosed section of path where Ash Copse borders the Coln, before reaching a second gate and a riverside meadow. Head directly across this field, the Coln meandering away to your left, to the far left corner. Pass through a gate, and continue along the riverbank for 150 yards to a distinct fork. Bear right, heading away from the river towards an area of

39

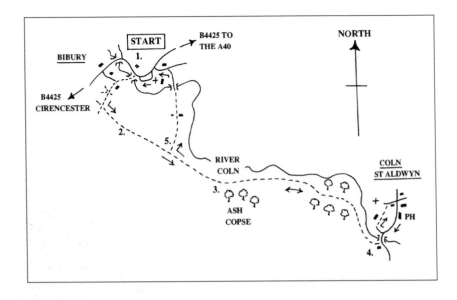

woodland. Continue along the edge of this woodland for 400 yards, and keep on the path as it bears right to pass through the woodland itself. Where the woodland path ends at a gate, keep directly ahead along a waterside meadow to a lodge on the far side of the field. Pass through two gates by this lodge to join the Coln St Aldwyn to Quenington road.

4. Turn left, cross the Coln and turn left to follow the lane leading to Mill House. Just past the entrance to Mill House, cross a footbridge on the right across the river and continue uphill along an enclosed footpath. This path shortly becomes a lane which very soon reaches a road junction, where a detour to the left will bring you to Coln St Aldwyn church. For the main walk, turn right, pass some almshouses and continue to a crossroads and a small green in the centre of the village, alongside the village store. Turn right, follow the Quenington road down past the New Inn – an obligatory refreshment stop – and continue along the road back to the River Coln and that lodge passed on first entering Coln St Aldwyn. Turn right, and retrace your steps for 1³/₄ miles back to that junction just outside Bibury.

5. Rather than turning left along the path followed at the beginning of the walk, keep on the main track as it bears right and passes

Arlington Row

through a gateway. Follow this track northwards across open countryside, the Coln across the fields on the right, towards a prominent house in the distance. On approaching this house, pass through another gateway and continue along a metalled lane that winds its way down past Bibury Mill. Cross the millstream and continue along the lane to its junction with the Bibury to Coln St Aldwyn road, Bibury Court being the attractive building on your left.

Turn left to reach the B4425, then left again back into Bibury. Very soon, pass through a gap in the wall on the left to join a lane by a telephone box. Follow this lane down past some cottages and the entrance to Bibury church. Continue along this lane as it bears right back to the B4425. Follow the main road back into the centre of Bibury.

PLACES OF INTEREST NEARBY

Not to be missed in Bibury is the *Arlington Mill Museum and Gallery*. Grindstones and mill machinery still turn, and the series of displays relate to life and work in the Cotswolds in years gone by. Telephone: 01285 740368.

THE RIVER LEACH AT SOUTHROP

✥

Step out along the River Leach as it charts a course between a trio of charming Cotswold villages. Lovely throughout the year, this route, with daffodils and willows along the way, is the perfect walk to welcome in springtime.

Eastleach Martin

The Leach, despite its lack of miles, is one of the best-loved of the Cotswold rivers. From its source at Hampnett, just above Northleach, the river flows for less than 20 miles to its confluence with the Thames at Lechlade. Along the way are a number of quite delightful Cotswold villages, typified by Southrop, Eastleach Turville and Eastleach Martin, whose lanes, churches and cottages add charm to this walk. Between the villages lie the willows and water meadows of the River Leach, where swallow and swift delight in the sun-warmed surface of the stream.

The walk sets out from Southrop, whose manor house, mill, cottages and diminutive church provide the visitor with archetypal

Cotswold architecture. Hidden at the end of a cul-de-sac lane, the church does take some finding but is well worth seeking out. Largely Norman, the fine font is what excites the interest of the guidebook writers. It is a quite excellent example of 12th-century craftsmanship, with its subjects ranging from 'Moses with the Tables of the Law' to 'The Virtues Trampling on the Vices'. John Keble, founder of the Oxford Movement, was curate at Southrop from 1823 to 1825, and it was in the nearby Old Vicarage that the first stirrings of the movement are thought to have taken place when Keble invited along friends from Oxford for 'reading parties' during vacations.

From Southrop, the meadows bordering the Leach are followed northwards to the neighbouring villages of Eastleach Turville and Eastleach Martin. The stone cottages and houses of these adjoining settlements quite literally face each other across the waters of the Leach, which are crossed along the way by means of a fine stone clapper bridge. Pass this way in early springtime, and the banks of the Leach are adorned by flowering daffodils, with the whole scene being one of the most photographed spots in the Cotswolds. It really is a most beautiful location, and is best enjoyed outside of weekends when day-trippers and their vehicles do rather detract from an otherwise quite beautiful scene. A quiet lane bordering the river is followed back to Coate Mill, before our steps quite literally follow a riverside path besides the sparking waters of the Leach before the walk returns to Southrop.

The creeper-covered walls of the Swan Inn in Southrop overlook a tiny green in the heart of the village. The low-ceilinged front bar, with its wooden tables and chairs and cottagey wall seats, presents visitors with a most traditional feel, which is further enhanced by exposed stonework, wooden beams and a welcoming open fire in winter. Adding to this feel are a number of prints and mirrors, hunting horns and tankards, which are displayed around the walls of this fine old Cotswold hostelry.

The Swan is best known for its varied and imaginative food. At one end of the menu are all the traditional favourites, for example sausage and chips and cottage pie, whilst more adventurous tastes might opt for such tempting selections as goat's cheese in puff pastry or buckwheat pancake filled with chicken, bacon and mushrooms. To accompany your meal, a number of fine real ales are available, which might typically include Morland Original and Archers Golden.

Should you be visiting the Swan on a fine summer's day, the sheltered garden behind the inn is a perfect spot to relax. Telephone: 01367 85205.

- **HOW TO GET THERE:** Initially, make for Fairford which lies between Cirencester and Lechlade on the A417. Just outside Fairford, on the Lechlade side of the town, follow the unclassified road that is signposted to Southrop. The village lies 3½ miles north-east of the A417, with the Swan Inn fronting onto the main street.
- **PARKING:** There is room for roadside parking on the village lanes in the vicinity of the Swan Inn. An ideal place to park is on the Eastleach Turville lane that runs alongside the inn.
- **LENGTH OF THE WALK:** 3½ miles. Maps: OS Landranger 163 Cheltenham and Cirencester and OS Outdoor Leisure 45 The Cotswolds (GR 200035).

THE WALK

1. Walk down the road in front of the Swan Inn, signposted to Filkins. Shortly, on the left, you pass the village school followed by Pear Tree Cottage. Immediately past this cottage, turn left along an almost hidden footpath that runs between cottages up to a stone slab stile. If you walk down the village street as far as the right turn to the church, you have gone too far! Cross the stile, and follow the fence ahead to a stile on the left. Continue along the bottom edge of a paddock to another stile, before continuing along the bottom of the next paddock to another stile by a telegraph pole. Head directly across the next – much larger – field towards a property some 250 yards distant, shown on the OS sheets as Coate Farm.

2. Cross the stile just before the property, cross the driveway leading to the farmhouse and enter the field opposite. Continue along the lower edge of this field, following the boundary wall alongside Coate Farm. In the corner of this field, cross a stile and a footbridge into the next field. Head across to the far right-hand corner of this field, keeping to the left of a paddock in the corner, to reach a gateway. In the next field, follow the line of trees directly ahead, a tributary stream of the Leach down below on the right. Where this line of trees ends, keep directly ahead to a gate and stile. Cross the next field to a yellow post opposite alongside a stile, before continuing down a footpath into Eastleach Turville.

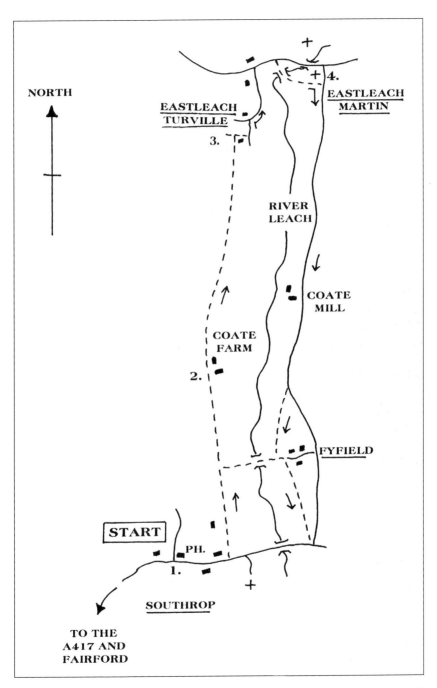

NORTH

EASTLEACH
TURVILLE

3.

EASTLEACH
MARTIN

4.

RIVER
LEACH

COATE
MILL

COATE
FARM

2.

FYFIELD

START

PH.

1.

SOUTHROP

TO THE
A417 AND
FAIRFORD

3. At a junction with a green lane, turn right by a cottage to reach a metalled lane. Follow this lane to the left to the next junction, before turning right to follow a lane around to the main road that runs between Eastleach Turville and Eastleach Martin. You should join this road directly opposite a war memorial. Turn right and, very shortly, cross a stone clapper bridge on the right across the Leach. Follow the path beyond this bridge that bears left alongside the river into Eastleach Martin churchyard. Pass to the right of the church, and on through a gate to join a quiet lane.

4. Follow this lane to the right, bordering the Leach for much of the way. In 1/2 mile, the lane passes Coate Mill. In another 200 yards, just before a left-hand bend, bear right off of the lane to follow a signposted footpath down to the banks of the Leach. Follow the riverbank downstream for 300 yards to a clapper bridge across the river. At this point, rather than crossing the Leach, turn left to follow a track up towards the hamlet of Fyfield. Just past a gateway, and just before reaching the hamlet, cross the grass on the right to enter the bottom corner of a field. (NB: There is no signpost or stile at this point. The barbed wire fence has been tied up to give walkers access to the field.) Having entered the field, follow the fence on the left uphill for 20 yards until, halfway up the hillside, you bear right to head directly across the middle of the field, following an uncultivated strip to a stile in the far corner of the field by a road junction. Turn right into Southrop, crossing the Leach along the way, and continue uphill back to the Swan Inn.

PLACES OF INTEREST NEARBY

The *Cotswold Wildlife Park* is 5 miles north-east of Southrop, on the A361 3 miles south of Burford. The wide variety of animals are located in 200 acres of gardens and parkland surrounding Bradwell Grove, an early 19th-century mansion in the Tudor style. Telephone: 01993 823006.

WALK 9
THE RIVER THAMES AT BUSCOT

Seemingly a million miles from the bustle of England's capital city, the Thames flows gently through a pastoral landscape just inside the Oxfordshire border. The intrusion of pleasure craft on the river only adds to what is a most picturesque setting.

Buscot Lock

This most delightful of riverside walks begins at Buscot, a National Trust village just downstream of Lechlade. This is very much the estate village of nearby Buscot Park which, although lying off the actual walk, is well worth a visit in its own right.

From Buscot, the walk heads across the fields to the neighbouring village of Kelmscot (variously spelt with one or two 't's). It is forever associated with the craftsman and poet William Morris. Morris lived in Kelmscot's Elizabethan manor from 1871 to his death in 1896, and his description of the place in a letter to a friend deserves repetition: 'I have been looking about for a house for the wife and kids, and whither do you guess my eye is turned now? Kelmscot, a little village about two mile above Radcot Bridge – a heaven on earth; an old stone Elizabethan house – and such a garden! close down on the river, a boat house, and all things handy . . .'

The return to Buscot quite literally follows the banks of the River Thames, at this point nearing the upper limits of its navigable water. Other than the delightful Kelmscot Navigation Bridge, its adjoining moorings and Buscot Weir Lock, there is little of a man-made nature to intrude on the landscape at this juncture. It is simply the Thames, that most majestic of our rivers, wending its way across what is a most English of landscapes – the river's course set against a backdrop of arable fields, pasture and woodland.

A convenient stopping-off point halfway around the walk is the Plough Inn at Kelmscot. The cottage-style hostelry fronts onto a delightful garden, where tables and chairs lie scattered amongst interesting floral displays. Internally, the Plough Inn has two bars for its customers. The front bar area has a most traditional feel, with its flagstones and exposed stonework, and adjoins a carpeted lounge bar, decorated with a selection of prints.

Lighter appetites will enjoy the Plough's sandwiches, filled French bread, soup, baked potatoes or ploughman's, whilst those of a hungrier disposition will be attracted by such dishes as ham and egg, beef and ale pie and cajun chicken. If energy levels need a further boost before the walk along the Thames back to Buscot, then one of the appetising desserts such as chocolate sponge or fruit fool will not go amiss. Fortified by a glass of Morland Original or Fuller's London Pride, walkers leaving the Plough Inn will feel well and truly refreshed. Telephone: 01367 253543.

- **HOW TO GET THERE:** Turn off the A417 between Lechlade and Faringdon in the village of Buscot, 2 miles east of Lechlade, taking the cul-de-sac lane that leads down to Buscot Weir.
- **PARKING:** A little way down the cul-de-sac lane described above, shortly after the village store, turn right and park in the NT's signposted Buscot Weir car park.
- **LENGTH OF THE WALK:** 5 miles. Maps: OS Landranger 163 Cheltenham and Cirencester and OS Explorer 169 Cirencester and Swindon (GR 231976).

THE WALK

1. Leave the car park and turn right to follow the lane down

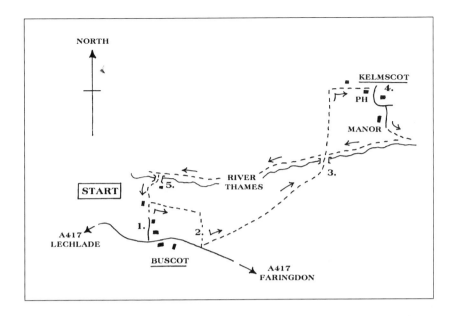

towards the River Thames. In 200 yards, where the lane enters a large green that borders the river, turn right. Follow the top end of this green to a footbridge in the corner. Cross this footbridge, before following the top right-hand edge of the adjoining field. On the far side of the field, pass through a gap by an electricity pole before following the left edge of the next field to a gate in the corner and a track. Turn right, and follow this track up to the main A417.

2. Just before the main road, turn left through a gateway to follow a signposted footpath which crosses a field diagonally to a gap in the far left-hand corner. Head directly across the middle of the next field to the large tree opposite, beneath which a footbridge is crossed which brings the path into the bottom corner of the next field. Turn right through a gap in the hedge, before turning left to follow the edge of the neighbouring field uphill along an uncultivated grass strip. Continue to the extreme left-hand corner of this field, cross a footbridge on the left and then cross to the far right-hand corner of the next field, where the path joins a track which leads to the River Thames. Follow this track to the entrance of the Anchor Boat Club, before continuing to the ornate wooden bridge that crosses the river.

3. Cross the Thames, turn right into the field bordering the river and then turn left to follow a fence away from the riverbank. At the top of this field, cross a stile and follow the hedgerow ahead, keeping the hedge to your right. At the top end of the field, turn right along a track into Kelmscot. Keep on this track until you emerge in Kelmscot by the Plough Inn.

4. Turn right, and follow the main village street – ignoring an immediate right turn that leads past a telephone box. In 150 yards, at the junction by a small green, turn right down the lane signposted to Kelmscot Manor. Continue down to the manor, beyond which keep on the unmetalled track which bears left down to the Thames. Just before the river, turn right across a footbridge over a tributary stream before following the river itself upstream – to the right – for 1½ miles back to Buscot.

5. As you approach Buscot, cross a bridge over the Thames to reach an island, turn right and cross the pasture to reach a stile at the far end, beyond which lies Buscot Lock. Cross the upper set of lock gates, and follow the path ahead over the footbridge above Buscot Weir and on around a cottage to reach a driveway. Follow this drive to the left, across the open green passed at the outset, and back up to the NT Buscot Weir car park.

PLACES OF INTEREST NEARBY

Buscot Park (NT) is a 55-acre park, with water gardens, a tree-fringed lake and a traditional walled kitchen garden. It also boasts a fine Adam-style house. Telephone: 01367 240786.

THE RIVER THAMES AT LECHLADE

Lechlade, Gloucestershire's only town on the Thames, has been described as a memorial to the craftsmen of the Cotswolds. The walk provides every opportunity to explore the attractive town centre as well as a river bustling with the sound and colour of pleasure craft.

Lechlade

Lechlade owes a good deal of its prosperity to the presence of rivers and waterways. The River Thames, whose navigable waters end just outside the town, is joined by both the Leach and the Coln within the town's boundaries. The Thames and Severn Canal also joined the Thames at Lechlade, which brought considerable trade to the waterways in the 18th and 19th centuries. As many as 100 barges could be seen tied up along the riverbank in times past, and it was at Lechlade that stone used in the dome of St Paul's Cathedral was loaded onto vessels bound for the capital.

To this day, there is much of interest along the riverside section of this walk. Halfpenny Bridge, just to the south of the town centre, is named after the toll once charged to cross the waterway, whilst the lock alongside St John's Bridge is the highest along the River Thames. Standing alongside St John's Lock is the well-known statue of Old Father Thames, originally carved back in 1851 for the Great Exhibition at Crystal Palace. The statue was subsequently placed at the source of the Thames near Kemble, but was removed to St John's Lock in 1974 on account of persistent vandalism in its isolated location at Thames Head.

This is a bustling section of the river, with a plethora of pleasure craft completing their journeys along the navigable section of the river. The moorings are always busy and occupied, with boat owners enjoying a few hours rest in the Gloucestershire countryside before resuming their journeys downstream. The river is equally popular with wildlife, with coot, moorhen, ducks and swans resident here in large numbers, together with dragonflies and damselflies.

Away from the river, the town of Lechlade has much to interest the visitor. The many fine 18th and 19th-century houses centred around the Market Square are an absolute delight, with the 15th-century church, topped by its magnificent spire, dominating the townscape. The footpath leading from St John's Bridge to the church has been named 'Shelley's Walk' on account of its appeal to the poet. It was in the churchyard at Lechlade in 1815 that Shelley was inspired to write his *Summer Evening Meditation*. His description of the church bears repetition:

> 'Thou, too, aerial pile, whose pinnacles
> Point from one shrine like pinnacles of fire.'

Almost at journey's end stands the Trout Inn, whose Thamesside garden remains ever popular with visitors. In summertime, a marquee is erected by the river, with a summer bar for customers. If you prefer to take refreshment indoors, you will discover a fine old inn that dates back to 1472. With its low beams, panelled walls and flagstones, the Trout Inn exudes a real sense of history. There are, of course, fishing prints around the walls, together with stuffed fish that include trout and pike, all of which can be enjoyed from traditional wooden tables and settles.

A good selection of well-presented food is available at the Trout Inn, including home-made soup, ploughman's and pizzas. More substantial dishes include seafood crumble, rump steak and locally made sausages. To accompany your meal, the beers include Courage Best and Directors, as well as John Smith's Bitter. On a summer's day, a riverside walk along Old Father Thames, combined with good food and drink in a Thamesside garden will surely prove irresistible. Telephone: 01367 252313.

- **HOW TO GET THERE:** The walk starts at a layby near the Trout Inn. The Trout Inn lies on the A417 Faringdon road, just 3/4 mile outside Lechlade, just to the west of St John's Bridge and the River Thames.
- **PARKING:** Just west of the Trout Inn, there is a layby opposite a garage and caravan park on the A417.
- **LENGTH OF THE WALK:** 3 miles. Maps: OS Landranger 163 Cheltenham and Cirencester and OS Explorer 169 Cirencester and Swindon (GR 223992).

THE WALK

1. Walk along the pavement besides the A417 towards the Trout Inn and, opposite the left turn to Kelmscot, turn right along the tarmac footpath – Shelley's Walk. Follow this enclosed path to a stile, before continuing across the field ahead, still on a tarmac path, towards Lechlade church. At the far side of the field, cross another stile, continue past the village school and on through Lechlade churchyard to the A417 in the centre of Lechlade.

2. Follow the main road ahead – the A417 road to Cirencester – to a layby on the edge of Lechlade on the left, in front of a number of houses. At the far end of this layby, just past a house called Burnside, turn left to cross a stile before following an enclosed path across four fields, clearly visible stiles marking the course of the right-of-way. In the corner of the fourth field, cross a stile to join a lane.

3. Turn left and, almost immediately, left again along a gravelled track signposted as a footpath. Follow this track for 400 yards until it becomes the private drive leading to a property called The Roundhouse, which overlooks the point where the Thames and Severn Canal joined the River Thames. At this point, fork left onto a signposted path that follows a short stretch of the River Coln to its confluence with the Thames.

53

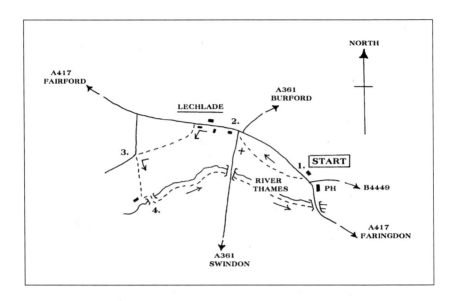

4. Cross the footbridge ahead over the Thames, turn left and follow the south bank of the river downstream for 1½ miles to St John's Bridge, passing beneath Halfpenny Bridge along the way. All the while, there are good views across the river towards Lechlade, with the spire of the parish church being the most prominent landmark. Just past St John's Lock, and the statue of Old Father Thames, climb the steps leading up to the A417. Turn left, cross the bridge and on the right is the Trout Inn. Just a short distance beyond the inn is the layby.

WALK 11

THE RIVER COLN AT FAIRFORD

Fairford is a welcoming little Cotswold town, with a broad main street that leads from the square to the magnificent 15th-century church. The view down to the water meadows alongside the Coln is quintessentially English, with Fairford Mill and the old bridge across the river forming a picture postcard setting.

Fairford Mill

The noted antiquary John Leland, Henry VIII's librarian, believed that 'Fairforde never flourished afore ye Tames came to it.' The prosperity of this small Cotswold town in late medieval times was undoubtedly due to the Tames, one of the Cotswold's greatest wool merchant families. The town's crowning glory, St Mary the Virgin church, was built by John Tame and his son Edmund. The remarkably complete series of stained glass windows, the work of the Fleming Barnard Flower, will surely catch the eye, but do not overlook the stone effigy of Tiddles the Church Cat, whose remains lie buried just outside the church porch.

Poor though Fairford would be without its fine Perpendicular church, it would surely be an altogether different place without the bright sparkling waters of the River Coln. Here the river is just a few miles above its confluence with the Thames at Lechlade, and much of the walk follows the Coln to the east of Fairford. Wildfowl make their home along this stretch of the river, with several species of duck, as well as coot and moorhen, being commonplace.

To the east of Fairford, our steps also follow the banks of a vast lake, a former gravel pit that is now yet another haven for wildfowl. Especially common hereabouts are Canada geese, introduced to Britain as 'ornamental wildfowl' from North America some 250 years ago. *Branta canadensis* can be over 3 feet in length, and utter a loud, distinctive 'a-honk' in flight or when alarmed.

Back in Fairford, the walk ends up in the town square – more properly known as the Market Place. A pleasing mixture of largely 17th and 18th-century buildings lie centred around the Bull Hotel. Historically, part of this building was a monks' chanting house, with another part being a hall for a local trade guild. In the 18th century, the Bull Hotel became a posting house on the Gloucester to London turnpike, and has remained a place of rest and refreshment ever since.

This imposing stone hostelry, whose inn sign depicts a magnificent Herefordshire bull, exudes a great sense of history and tradition. Low ceilings, beams and open fireplaces give a very real feeling of stepping back in time, to an era illustrated by a number of pictures, prints and maps that are displayed around the walls. The Bull offers a range of food that includes sandwiches, jacket potatoes and ploughman's, as well as light meals, fish dishes and 'Bull fare'. The fish dishes include trout stuffed with Stilton as well as traditional fish and chips, whilst the Bull fare includes lamb noisettes and Indonesian diced lamb. To accomany your meal, a pint of Arkell's 3B or Kingsdown brewed in nearby Swindon would not go amiss. Telephone: 01285 712535.

- ● **HOW TO GET THERE/PARKING:** Fairford lies 8 miles east of Cirencester on the A417 road to Lechlade. Turn off the main road in the centre of the town to park in the Market Place, on the western side of which lies the Bull Hotel. If there is no room for parking in the Market Place, then continue up the High Street to the car park just above the church.

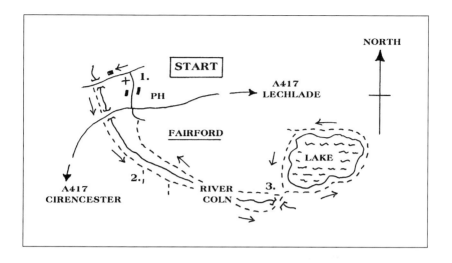

● **LENGTH OF THE WALK:** 4 miles, including 1 mile around the lake. Maps: OS Landranger 163 Cheltenham and Cirencester and OS Explorer 169 Cirencester and Swindon (GR 152011).

THE WALK

1. Walk up the High Street past St Mary the Virgin church to a road junction, and turn left into Mill Lane. Follow Mill Lane downhill to Mill Bridge, cross the Coln and continue along the road for another 50 yards to Pitham Brook. Cross the brook, and immediately cross a stone slab stile on the left. Follow Pitham Brook downstream back into Fairford, enjoying all the while fine views on the left of the Coln, the mill and Fairford church. At the far side of the field, cross a stile and continue along an enclosed stretch of path that runs between houses down to the A417. Cross over into Waterloo Lane, and follow this lane along to Waterloo Cottage. Beyond this property, continue along what becomes a tarmac path that heads out of Fairford, the Coln hidden behind the hedgerow on the left.

2. In ¼ mile, by a wooden fence, the path forks. Bear left, and follow the waymarked path down to a bungalow on the left-hand side of the path. Continue past this property along a driveway, very soon passing a large detached property on the left. At this point, the main drive bears right. The walk, however, passes through a gateway on the left, before bearing right to follow a gravelled access drive past an assortment of cottages and farm buildings. Pass to the right of one final cottage – literally through a side garden – to reach a stile and open fields. Bear left across the first field, the Coln on the left, to reach a stile at the far end of the field. In the next field, follow the top right-hand edge alongside Cleeve Wood, the Coln below on the left. Where the wood ends, keep directly ahead for 30 yards to reach a stile in the far left corner of the field. Cross this stile, and the footbridge beyond, before continuing through an area of scrub on a path that leads to a footbridge across the River Coln.

3. Cross the river, and turn left to follow the Coln upstream. In just 10 yards, an almost obligatory detour presents itself. Cross the footbridge on the right to enter an enclosure containing a flooded gravel pit. The circumference of this lake is close on 1 mile. Turn right, and follow the path all the way around the lakeside, returning eventually to that footbridge and the banks of the Coln. Continue following the river upstream – to the right – back towards Fairford. In $3/4$ mile, the riverside path reaches a footbridge that crosses the river on the left. At this point, keep directly ahead, following a path that bears slightly right away from the river and between some houses. In 150 yards, at a junction, turn left along Back Lane to reach the A417. Cross over into Fairford's Market Place.

PLACES OF INTEREST NEARBY
To the east of Fairford lies the Fairford/Lechlade section of the *Cotswold Water Park*. A series of flooded gravel pits, of varying ages, depths and sizes, has been developed into a major recreational resource offering many forms of water sports including sailing, water skiing and fishing. Because of the alkaline gravels, the water is itself alkaline in character. It is exceptionally pure and supports a range of aquatic fauna and flora.

WALK 12

THE COTSWOLD WATER PARK
NEAR SOUTH CERNEY

The Cotswold Water Park has been described as the Lake District of the South. Flooded gravel pits have created over 75 lakes in the 10 miles of countryside lying between Kemble and Cricklade.

One of the many lakes at the Park

The Cotswold Water Park (West), just a few miles south of Cirencester, comprises a surprising number of lakes in a diminutive swathe of countryside that stretches from Kemble eastwards to Cricklade. The lakes, resulting from gravel extraction in the Upper Thames Valley, now provide one of the region's fastest growing leisure facilities, with activities as diverse as bird-watching and sailing, fishing and jet-skiing available for visitors.

Our exploration of the western section of the Water Park begins in South Cerney, a picturesque Cotswold village on the banks of the River Churn. It is now more than 60 years since Arthur Mee, in his

King's England guide to Gloucestershire, penned an eloquent description of South Cerney: 'Here flows the Churn, tributary of the Thames, singing its way past cottage doors and giving its name to the village – Churney. Very beautiful is the village with its stream, its thatched and tiled cottages with their dormer windows, its houses of Cotswold stone, and its noble church with much treasure from far-off days.'

Adding to the watery theme of this walk is the long disused Thames and Severn Canal. Opened in 1798 to link the Stroudwater Canal at Stroud with the Thames at Lechlade, the Thames and Severn was never a great success. The canal was finally abandoned in 1927, leaving little more than a muddy ditch stretching across the Gloucestershire countryside.

As with all fine walks, this excursion into the Gloucestershire countryside includes a visit to a fine hostelry. The Eliot Arms in South Cerney, a 16th-century stone inn, is a three-storey building with a splendid creeper climbing towards its gabled roof. The inn certainly lives up to its historic origins, with exposed stonework, beams, cosy alcoves and stone fireplaces. It is comfortably furnished with captain's chairs, built-in corner seats, pew seats and bar-stools, whilst picnic tables in the rear garden provide an idyllic spot to enjoy refreshment during the warmer parts of the year. Many items of memorabilia are displayed around the bar area, including carpentry tools, stirrups, old bottles, plates and motor-racing prints.

A wide range of bar food is available at the inn, from lighter, less expensive snacks, through to substantial meals that will certainly counteract the benefit of any calories you may lose on this waterside walk! From sandwiches, filled baked potatoes and ploughman's, through to lamb and apricot pie, home-made salmon fishcakes and duck with an orange and cointreau sauce, there is something on the menu to satisfy every possible taste.

The Eliot Arms will also provide a tipple to satisfy the thirsts of most drinkers. Beers and ales include Boddingtons, Flowers Original and Wadworth 6X, as well as a range of foreign bottle beers. Beyond this, over 100 malt whiskies are available for connoisseurs of something just a little stronger. Telephone: 01285 860215.

- **HOW TO GET THERE:** An unclassified road leads from Kemble, on the A429 south of Cirencester, through Ewen to South Cerney. You can also approach from the A419 Cirencester-Swindon road. In the

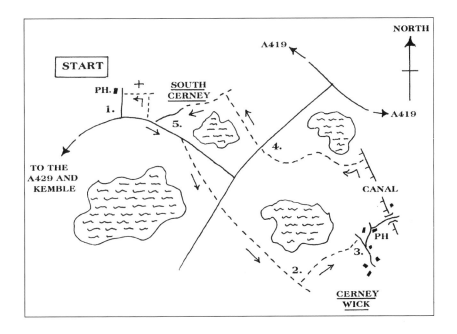

centre of South Cerney, turn by the village cross into Clarks Hay.
The Eliot Arms lies 150 yards along Clarks Hay, on the left-hand
side.

- **PARKING:** There is plenty of room for roadside parking in Clarks
  Hay, in the vicinity of the Eliot Arms.
- **LENGTH OF THE WALK:** 5 miles. Maps: OS Landranger 163
  Cheltenham and Cirencester and OS Explorer 169 Cirencester and
  Swindon (GR 048972).

THE WALK

1. Walk down Clarks Hay to the junction by the village cross before
turning left along Station Road, the road signposted to Cricklade.
Follow this road for 3/4 mile until, just outside South Cerney, you
turn right onto a bridleway signposted to Cricklade. Follow this path
for 1/2 mile to Spine Road, passing between lakes along the way.
Cross Spine Road by a brick bridge and continue along the
bridleway.

2. In just over 1/2 mile, cross a stile on the left onto a path
signposted to Cerney Wick Lakes. Follow the right edge of a

61

paddock, a lake to the left, to a footbridge in the corner. Beyond this bridge, follow the path to the right of the lake ahead. The path bears right and then left around the end of the lake before reaching a stile in the corner of the enclosure. Follow the path across two small fields to a lane, emerging alongside a cottage.

3. Turn right and, at the next junction, left through Cerney Wick. In 100 yards, just past the Crown, turn right along the lane to Down Ampney. In 150 yards, turn left along a path – the Thames and Severn towpath – signposted to South Cerney. Follow the towpath for ½ mile before turning left onto a path signposted to the Churn. Walk along the end of the lake ahead, before bearing right to follow the lake's west bank. On the left is the River Churn. Continue following the path beside the Churn for 600 yards until emerging onto Spine Road (East).

4. Turn left, cross the Churn, then right into the local Education Centre. Follow the driveway in front of the Sports Centre, then continue along a grassy area beside the lake. Where the grass ends, continue along a grassy path, past a gateway to a junction. Continue along the left-hand path, which shortly borders another lake, separated by a fence. Keep on this path until it bears right to join Wildmoorway Lane. Turn left, and follow this lane back down to the road on the edge of South Cerney.

5. Follow the road to the right for ¼ mile. Just past The Lennards, turn right onto an enclosed path between houses. Follow this path up to the Churn, turn left and follow a lane called Bow Wow which joins the main road in South Cerney opposite the Eliot Arms.

WALK 13

THE SOURCE OF THE THAMES ABOVE KEMBLE

There is something special about discovering the source of a river, especially when that river is Old Father Thames. In a secluded field in the heart of Gloucestershire, a stone tablet marks the spot where the Thames begins its long journey down through Oxford and Reading to London. A romantic walk that will warm the heart of all true Englishmen!

The River Thames at Kemble

For most of the year, the source of the River Thames at Thames Head near Kemble is something of a disappointment. Other than a slight depression in the ground and a commemorative granite slab, the only water in the vicinity lies in a nearby cattle trough. Even the course of the river in its upper reaches is usually little more than a dry ditch, with the actual source being a spring that lies deep underground. Following periods of heavy rainfall, however, an altogether different sight awaits the visitor. The water table reaches the surface, the depression becomes a small pond, the springwater can be seen bubbling to the surface and a not insignificant stream flows across the fields towards Kemble and Ewen. A stirring sight for the true-blooded English person!

Even if the upper reaches of the Thames are dry, this walk explores a section of Thames and Severn Canal, another fascinating stretch of water. Just above the source of the Thames, this canal plunges into a deep cutting before reaching the Sapperton Tunnel. This 3,817 yard tunnel, the third longest canal tunnel in Britain, pierces the Cotswold escarpment. The ornate eastern portal is classical in style, and consists of 'a central pediment with flanking classical columns and finials, two niches, plus two circular and a rectangular entablature'.

Along this section of the Thames and Severn Canal lies a ruinous roundhouse, built between 1790 and 1791 to house the canal's lengthmen. These unique constructions were built of stone with stucco rendering, and the three-storey dwellings contained stables at ground level with the living-room and bedroom being housed on the upper two storeys.

If all of this is not sufficient to tempt you out into the Gloucestershire countryside, then the Tunnel House Inn, located in remote woodland above the canal tunnel, is worth visiting in its own right. It offers a range of basic bar food at value for money prices. Ploughman's or burgers, gala pie or cottage pie, perhaps chicken in a barbecue sauce – there will certainly be something on offer to cater for hungry appetites at the halfway point on this waterside walk. To accompany your meal, some excellent real ales are available that typically include Archers Best, Morland Old Speckled Hen, Young's and Wadworth 6X.

One of the best things about the Tunnel House Inn is its location, at the end of an unmetalled lane on the fringes of mature woodland. It was to this remote spot that upwards of 200 West Country and Derbyshire miners were brought to construct the Sapperton Tunnel, with this isolated bow-fronted stone house being their accommodation. If the navvies were to return today, they would feel completely at home. The Tunnel House Inn has made few concessions to the renovation mania that has afflicted so many pubs in Britain. With its unsophisticated food, fine real ales and eccentric decor, it continues to plough its own furrow! Telephone: 01285 770280.

- **HOW TO GET THERE/PARKING:** The walk begins from the car park on the London-bound side of Kemble Station. Turn off the A433 Cirencester-Tetbury road, 4 miles south-west of Cirencester, and follow the unclassified road signposted to Kemble. The turning is just south of the Thames Head Inn. As you enter Kemble, take the first turning on the right, an unsignposted road that leads into the car park (fee payable).
- **LENGTH OF THE WALK:** 6½ miles. Maps: OS Landranger 163 Cheltenham and Cirencester and OS Explorer 168 Stroud, Tetbury and Malmesbury (GR 985976).

THE WALK

1. Return to the road, turn left and continue out of Kemble for ³/₄ mile to the A433. Cross with care, and follow the lane signposted to Tarlton. In 1¼ miles, at the crossroads in Tarlton, follow the no through road opposite, signposted to the church. In 300 yards, a gravel track on the left leads to the small Norman church. About 50 yards beyond this turning, just past a cottage, follow the signposted footpath on the right.

2. Follow this path across the first field to a stile opposite. In the next field, drop down to a stone stile in the bottom right corner, before turning left in a third field to reach another stone stile in the corner. Beyond this stile, follow an uncultivated strip uphill in one final field, leading across to the Tunnel House Inn. Just past the inn, descend a stepped path on the right down to the Thames and Severn Canal and the Sapperton Tunnel. Follow the canal away from the tunnel for 1 mile, passing beneath a road bridge and a railway bridge before reaching Trewsbury Bridge.

3. Just before Trewsbury Bridge, follow the path on the right up to a track. Turn right along this track – signposted to Kemble – and continue to a gate. Then follow the left edge of three fields alongside woodland. Halfway across the third field, a stone on the left marks the source of the Thames. Cross to a gate on the far side of this third field, follow a line of trees across the next field to a gate, and in the next field, cross to a stile in the far right corner to reach the A433.

4. Cross the A433 to a stile opposite, before crossing a large field to

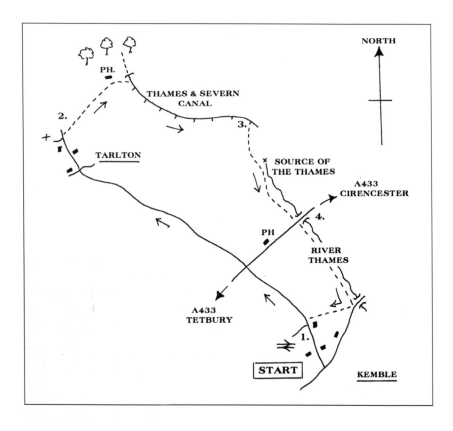

a gate in the far right corner. All the while, the Thames lies in the dip on the left. Cross the next field to reach a footbridge crossing a tributary stream of the Thames. Turn right, and follow this tributary to a stile. Follow the fence across the next field to a gate and a lane. Turn left, and the next right returns you to the car park.

PLACES OF INTEREST NEARBY

In nearby Cirencester, there is much to detain the visitor. The impressive turf-covered *Roman amphitheatre* is one free attraction. Full information on Cirencester can be obtained from the Tourist Information Centre on 01285 654180.

WALK 14
THE THAMES AND SEVERN CANAL
BELOW SAPPERTON

The view down through the Golden Valley below Sapperton will be an abiding memory from this waterside walk in the Cotswolds. Steep, wooded hillsides plunge down to the banks of the diminutive river Frome and the slowly decaying remains of the Thames and Severn Canal.

The Thames and Severn Canal, which opened to traffic in 1798, linked the Stroudwater Canal at Stroud with the head of the navigable River Thames at Inglesham near Lechlade. Deep in the Golden Valley above Stroud, the Thames and Severn is slowly reverting to nature, with occasional stretches of water lurking in the depths of what in mid-summer resembles primeval forest. The last recorded passage along this waterway was in 1911, although it was not until 1927 that the canal was finally abandoned.

The walk joins the Thames and Severn Canal at the former Oak Inn, deep in the valley below Frampton Mansell. Along the next 2 miles of what is a pleasant towpath walk through traditional English woodland, no fewer than nine locks lie in various states of decay before our steps reach the western portal of the Sapperton Tunnel. The tunnel's $2^1/_4$ miles of subterranean passageway make this one of the longest tunnels on Britain's canal network.

High above this secluded and secretive valley lie two fine Cotswold villages. Sapperton is situated on the divide between the agricultural uplands of the Cotswolds and the industrial valleys around Stroud. The highlight in the village is without doubt St Kenelm's church, where amongst the monuments is one to Sir Henry Poole, whose family held the patronage of the living from the 15th century onwards. On the hilltop to the south of the Golden Valley lies Frampton Mansell, often compared with an Alpine village. In the depths of winter, when snow is lying on the local hills, this is an apt description, especially given the Italian-style church in the heart of the village.

Just before reaching the imposing portal of the Sapperton Tunnel, the towpath passes the Daneway Inn. The Daneway was built in 1784 by John Nock, contractor for the Thames and Severn Canal. The building originally housed West Country and Derbyshire miners, who migrated to this remote Cotswold location to work on the tunnel's construction. Entering the Daneway really is like stepping back in time, with the bar containing a most imposing stone fireplace, whilst the walls are lined with elaborately carved oak that stretches from floor to ceiling. On a warm summer's day, however, most visitors prefer to relax on the sloping lawn that overlooks the former canal bed and the diminutive river Frome.

A good range of bar food is available at the Daneway, from soup, baps and ploughman's through to heartier dishes that might include beef and ale pie, steaks, lasagne and gammon and egg. To accompany your meal, a glass of Wadworth 6X comes highly recommended, as does a pint of Adnams Best or perhaps a local farmhouse cider. The only point to bear in mind is that from the Daneway, it is a not inconsiderable 250 foot climb uphill to the end of the walk in Sapperton. At least this exertion will provide the opportunity to work off a few of those calories taken on board at one of the Cotswold's most noted hostelries. Telephone: 01285 760297.

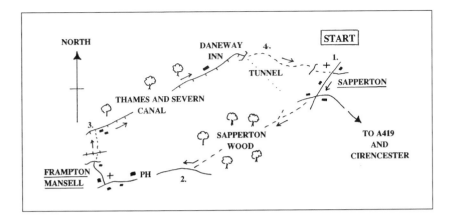

- **HOW TO GET THERE:** Turn off the A419 Cirencester-Stroud road, 4 miles west of Cirencester, and follow an unclassified turning signposted to Sapperton. Turn right into the village along the lane that passes the village school, and continue past the school as far as the church.
- **PARKING:** There is room for roadside parking on the cul-de-sac lane that runs above St Kenelm's church.
- **LENGTH OF THE WALK:** 4 miles. Maps: OS Landranger 163 Cheltenham and Cirencester and OS Explorer 168 Stroud, Tetbury and Malmesbury (GR 948033).

THE WALK

1. With your back to the church, follow the lane to the right through the village, passing the school, until you reach a junction by a green. Turn right along the road signposted to the Daneway and, in just a few yards, bear left along a signposted footpath into Sapperton Wood. Follow the main woodland path downhill to a clearing, at the far end of which the path joins a crosstrack. Turn left, and keep on the main woodland path for ³/₄ mile until you join the Frampton Mansell road.

2. Turn right, and follow this quiet hilltop lane for ¹/₂ mile into the village of Frampton Mansell. Just past the bus shelter and the telephone box, bear right downhill along the lane signposted to Oakridge. In 200 yards, at a junction, follow the enclosed footpath opposite – slightly to the right – which drops downhill to a stile and the main Stroud to London railway line. Cross the tracks WITH EXTREME CARE to a stile opposite, before continuing down the steep hillside to another stile just to the left of a cottage. Join a track, turn right and pass through the handgate ahead to follow a signposted footpath. You are now following the towpath of the disused Thames and Severn Canal.

3. Follow the canal up through the Golden Valley for 1½ miles, crossing a wooden footbridge after a mile or so to change banks, until you reach the lane by the Daneway Inn. Turn right, cross the bridge over the canal bed, and immediately turn left to follow the signposted footpath. This is still the canal towpath. Follow the canal bed for ¼ mile to the western entrance to Sapperton Tunnel.

4. Follow the path over the top of the tunnel portal to a stile. Bear half right uphill across a hillside field to a stile at the top of the field, cross this stile and continue along an enclosed path which soon bears right to join a lane. Cross over, and follow the path opposite uphill to a second lane, where a left turn will bring you back to the roadside parking by St Kenelm's church.

PLACES OF INTEREST NEARBY
Cirencester is home to the *Corinium Museum*, which chronicles the life and times of the Romans in the neighbourhood (telephone: 01285 655611). For more information about the town, refer to Walk 13.

WALK 15

THE THAMES AND SEVERN CANAL DEEP IN THE GOLDEN VALLEY

The towpath alongside the Thames and Severn Canal above Chalford passes through a landscape that has barely altered over the last 200 years. Steep wooded hillsides tumble down towards the valley bottom, where the only signs of human habitation are the stone cottages that date from the 17th and 18th centuries. This is truly a secluded and isolated corner of the Cotswolds.

The reservoir that has now become a popular nature reserve

The valleys in and around Stroud represent perhaps the most industrialised parts of the Cotswolds. Fortunately, the region's wealth was based upon the textile industry, not heavy industry such as engineering or steel. This has left a legacy of attractive stone mills and weavers' cottages, rather than decaying iron works and slag heaps, which does lend these valleys a certain charm.

To the east of Stroud lies the Golden Valley, a fine description of

71

the local landscape during the autumn months, when the wooded hillsides turn a beautiful copper-gold colour. Deep in the valley lie very contrasting stretches of water – the diminutive river Frome on its journey to the river Severn from its source above Sapperton, and the Thames and Severn Canal which links what are arguably the greatest rivers in England.

The towpath alongside the Thames and Severn Canal initially passes through the village of Chalford. This hillside settlement, dating from the very early years of the Industrial Revolution, soon spread itself across the south-facing slopes of the Golden Valley. Chalford is a delightful collection of 18th and 19th-century cottages and dwellings that are scattered along the network of steep lanes and alleyways that lie above the valley bottom, where the River Frome provided power for the local woollen mills. Such is the steepness of these hillside byways that, well into the 20th century, panniered donkeys were used to deliver goods.

It is not too long before the towpath leaves Chalford behind, and passes out into the unique rural landscape that is the Golden Valley, a secluded corner of Gloucestershire that genuinely does possess a character all of its own. The Thames and Severn Canal and the neighbouring River Frome follow each other along the bottom of the valley, a scene that has hardly altered at all since the navigators carved out the waterway's course. Along the way lies the occasional ruinous lock chamber before the walk reaches a delightful lake immediately above Baker's Mill.

Away from the confines of the valley, the walk follows the hillsides to the south where, in addition to expansive views across to Oakridge on the opposite hilltop, there is a pleasant stroll through the shady confines of Cowcombe Wood. High on the hilltop lies Frampton Mansell, a small village with a handsome neo-Norman church and a welcoming hostelry called the Crown Inn. Constructed of local Cotswold stone, the Crown fronts onto a lawn with a good number of picnic tables. Internally, there is a friendly lounge bar, with exposed stonework, flagstones and a dark beam-and-plank ceiling. It is altogether a picture.

A good range of bar food is available, as well as meals in the inn's restaurant. Whether your forte is light snacks such as sandwiches, soup or ploughman's, or more substantial offerings such as salads, chicken, steak or fish dishes, the menu will be sure to satisfy that appetite built up on the climb from the canal down in the valley bottom. To go with your meal, a number of fine West Country beers are available at the Crown which typically include Oakhill Farmers, Archers Village and Wadworth 6X. In fine weather, enjoy your refreshment in the garden, with its views over the village and towards the Golden Valley. The only regret that I have heard voiced hereabouts is that the sound of steam trains can no longer be heard on the former GWR Stroud to London railway down in the valley. The nostalgic sound of a bygone era has been replaced by the rather more functional diesel engine! Telephone: 01285 760601.

- **HOW TO GET THERE/PARKING:** Approaching from Cirencester, follow the A419 west for 8 miles towards Stroud. Just before the main road begins its steep descent into the Golden Valley, park in the large layby on the northern side of the road, opposite the Cotswold Gliding Club.
- **LENGTH OF THE WALK:** 4 miles. Maps: OS Landranger 163 Cheltenham and Cirencester and OS Explorer 168 Stroud, Tetbury and Malmesbury (GR 911019).

THE WALK

1. Walk to the western end of the layby, and continue along a lane that bears right down the hillside. In 100 yards, at a minor crossroads, turn left up to the A419. Cross the main road with care, and follow the lane opposite for 150 yards to a junction. Follow the bridleway opposite for $^1/_2$ mile. Initially, it follows an enclosed course, before following the right edge of a field. Just over halfway across this field, pass through a gateway on the right – actually a gap in the wall with a missing gate – before following the right edge of a field down to Cowcombe Wood.

2. Enter the woodland, and follow the bridleway to the left. Keep on this track as it shortly bears right downhill to a junction. Turn right and, in a short distance, left to continue on the woodland path downhill to a gate and the A419. Cross to the pavement opposite, turn left and follow the main road downhill for 150 yards. Opposite the entrance to Springfield House, turn right to follow a signposted footpath. This is actually the towpath of the Thames and Severn Canal. Follow the towpath for $1^3/_4$ miles, passing beneath overbridges after $^1/_2$ mile and $1^1/_2$ miles.

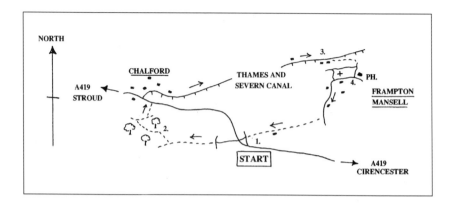

3. Just ¼ mile beyond the second overbridge, cross the canal bed on a small stone bridge beyond a lake, formerly the canal's reservoir. Bear left in front of a cottage and, in a few yards, follow the right-hand track beyond a stone outbuilding that climbs away from the canal to a gate and stile. Continue uphill along a green path to a second gate and stile at the top of the field. In the next field, turn right to a gate and cross the main London railway line WITH CARE. Continue on up the lane beyond the railway to a junction, before turning left up to another junction alongside the Crown Inn in Frampton Mansell.

4. Having enjoyed suitable refreshment, turn right and follow the Stroud road through the village. About 150 yards past the edge of Frampton Mansell, just past a house on the left called Four Ways, turn right along a signposted bridleway. Follow this bridleway for ¾ mile across the hilltop, enjoying the fine views across the Golden Valley on the right. Along the way, the path passes to the right of a collection of farm buildings. At the far end of the bridleway, beyond a gate, a lane is joined. Turn left, and follow this lane back uphill to the parking area besides the A419.

PLACES OF INTEREST NEARBY
At the end of the walk, it is worth driving the 6 miles down into Stroud to visit the *Stroud Museum* in Lansdown Hall. Amongst the many displays of local interest is one that details the history of the local cloth industry.

WALK 16

THE RIVER AVON AT MALMESBURY

Malmesbury claims to be the oldest borough in England, with its charter having been granted by Alfred the Great in AD 880. The ancient town sits proudly on a hilltop, surrounded by the Sherston and Tetbury branches of the Bristol Avon.

Malmesbury, seen from across the Avon

Whilst the purists will no doubt question Malmesbury's right to be classed as a Cotswold town, the local guidebooks all refer to this quiet corner of North Wiltshire as being on the Cotswold fringes. The buildings are certainly constructed of that golden limestone, whilst the town sits at the confluence of two Cotswold tributaries that both vie for the title of 'Source of the Avon'. The OS sheets obviously cannot decide, and refer to one as the 'River Avon (Tetbury branch)' and the other as the 'River Avon (Sherston branch)'.

The Avon was instrumental in Malmesbury's early prosperity, with the town developing as a weaving centre between the 15th and 18th centuries. The market cross at the top of the High Street dates from this period, as do the almshouses alongside St John's Bridge. The finest monument to this period in the town's history, however, is the former four-storey cloth mill just below St John's Bridge.

Dominating the town's skyline is the abbey, founded in the 7th century by St Aldhelm. A vast tower, standing some 445 feet high, collapsed in the 15th century, destroying much of the eastern end of the abbey, but what remains is still one of the best examples of Norman ecclesiastical church architecture in England. There is an interesting stained glass window in the abbey dedicated to Elmer, an 11th-century monk. Elmer jumped off the abbey tower adorned with home-made wings, but his futile attempts at flying left him crippled for life.

Away from the architecture of this delightful old town, there is every opportunity to explore both branches of the River Avon. The Tetbury branch passes through Conygre Mead Nature Reserve, whilst the Sherston branch flows through lush meadow land to the south of the town, with fine views up the hill towards the abbey itself. It is easy to see why this waterway system made Malmesbury into a virtual island, natural defences that were later fortified to offer the town additional protection.

A little way up the High Street at journey's end lies the Smoking Dog ... and what an unusual sign adorns the hostelry. This Cotswold stone inn fronts onto the main street, literally sandwiched between a rank of terraced cottages. Wooden floors, exposed stonework and traditional beams lend a rustic feel to the bar area. A passageway leads through to the dining area, whilst to the rear of the Smoking Dog is a small garden, just the place to relax with a pint during the summer months.

The Smoking Dog has earned a deserved reputation for its ever-changing menu and fine choice of food. The main menu rarely disappoints, and extends from baguettes and soup through to more substantial offerings such as courgette, mushroom and pepper filled pancakes and a duo of sausage kebabs chargrilled with spicy tomato sauce. A good range of real ales is usually available, beers that might include Smiles and Archers brews, as well as Wadworth 6X and Fuller's. Telephone: 01666 825823.

- **HOW TO GET THERE:** Malmesbury lies on the A429 road midway between Cirencester and Chippenham, with prominent road signs indicating the route to the town centre.

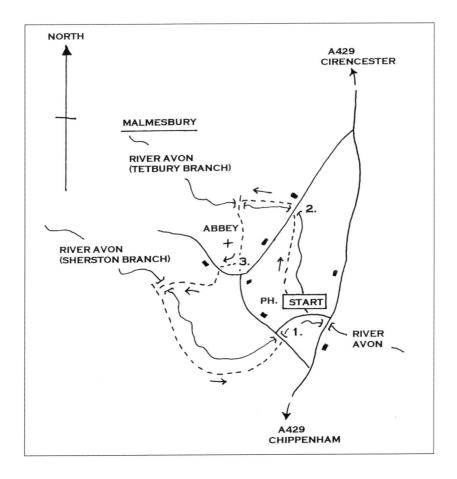

- **PARKING:** Follow the A429 to its junction with the B4042 road to Swindon. Leave the roundabout at this junction and follow the road signposted to the town centre. Immediately past St John's Bridge and the River Avon, turn right into St John's Street, where there is room for roadside parking.
- **LENGTH OF THE WALK:** 2 miles. Maps: OS Landranger 173 Swindon and Devizes and OS Explorer 168 Stroud, Tetbury and Malmesbury (GR 937870).

THE WALK
1. Walk along St John's Street away from the main road, cross a millstream and pass the local bowling club, before turning left along

a path that runs along the far side of the bowling green to a footbridge and a stile. Beyond this stile, head directly across a field to a stile and, in the next field, follow the River Avon on the right to another stile and the main road.

2. Turn right, cross the Avon and turn immediately left to follow a path beside the river alongside the Duke of York pub car park. This path shortly reaches a wooden gate and the entrance to the Conygre Mead Nature Reserve. Continue following the River Avon through the reserve until, at a fork, you keep right to follow a path above the river through to a car park. Turn left, and follow the footpath over the river up to the town centre, keeping left at the first junction to climb some steps up towards the abbey. At the top of these steps, follow a lane by the abbey through to the market cross.

3. Turn right by the market cross and the entrance to the abbey to follow Birdcage Walk. On reaching the main road, cross to the pavement opposite and turn left. Almost immediately, on a bend, turn right downhill along a narrow alleyway. Shortly, bear right down a flight of steps before continuing along a path on the right called Burnivale, which passes above a new housing development. Just past the new housing, turn left along an alleyway before crossing a series of bridges across the river to reach the water meadows. Follow the paved path to a clapper bridge, cross the river and turn left to pass through a gap at the end of a wall. Follow the left-hand field boundary across two fields, a little above the river. At the far side of the second field, continue along the riverbank towards the main road and Avon Mill. Just before the main road, cross the footbridge and continue along the pavement to the first turning on the right – St John's Street. If you continue up the main road for a short distance, the Smoking Dog is on the right-hand side.

PLACES OF INTEREST NEARBY

Although not literally on Malmesbury's doorstep, it is only half an hour's drive from the town into *Swindon*, where the *GWR Museum* and the *Railway Village Museum* are a must for visitors wishing to discover the history of a town that grew up around the Great Western Railway. Telephone: 01793 493189.

WALK 17

THE INFANT RIVER AVON NEAR LUCKINGTON

Finding the source of a river is always an exciting moment. Deep in the Southern Cotswolds lie a number of possible sources of the Bristol Avon, including the secluded Crow Down Springs, encountered on this walk.

Sherston

The River Avon flows down to those great cities of Bath and Bristol by way of Bradford-on-Avon, Chippenham and Malmesbury. Above Malmesbury, the river divides into what the official maps label as the Tetbury branch and the Sherston branch of the River Avon. It is on the Sherston branch that we find what might be classed as proper sources of a river, locations where it is clear that a river has its origins. The residents of Didmarton would like to claim that their village gives birth to the Avon. There on the edge of the village is Joyce's Pool, complete with a sign announcing to all and sundry that this is the source of the Avon. Sadly, the watercourses that flow downstream of this pond are usually dry ditches.

Venture a mile or so below Joyce's Pool, however, and we come to Crow Down Springs. A series of springs in the valley bottom consistently produce a flow of water, giving birth to the river that adds such beauty and delight to both Bath and Bristol.

Away from the diminutive watercourse that forms the focus for this walk, our steps also pass through three quite delightful Cotswold villages. The walk begins in Luckington, where several roads converge on the village green, which is overlooked by the Old Ship Inn. Whilst this part of the village might have lost a little of its attractiveness due to the network of passing roads, below in a tributary valley of the River Avon (Sherston branch) lies the more attractive older part of the village. Here we find the church, the faded apricot walls of Luckington Manor, Luckington Court, a group of farm buildings and the stone-tiled roofs of the rectory. It really is a delightful spot, reminiscent of all that is good about Cotswold architecture.

North of Luckington lies Sopworth, a smaller village but yet again a settlement that displays all the best features of Cotswold architecture. This is a farming community, with several fine stone barns, as well as delightful cottages, a manor house and the village church. In the shallow valley below Sopworth, our steps reach Crow Down Springs and the infant River Avon, before we pass the fringes of Sherston, the final village along the way. It is worth making a detour to visit the centre of Sherston, where you will find a broad main street, at one time the site of a market, overlooked by some quite exceptional 17th and 18th-century properties. There is also a rather fine church, with a somewhat dilapidated statue of one John Rattlebone. Rattlebone fought bravely against the Danes in a battle back in 1016, and was later awarded the Manor of Sherston. Today, Rattlebone is best known for giving his name to one of the village hostelries.

Back in Luckington, the Old Ship Inn presents a striking appearance with maroon paintwork contrasting with the cream walls of this 17th-century hostelry. Inside the Old Ship is a welcoming and comfortable bar area with a dining room extension. Perhaps of rather more interest in summer months is the inn's garden, where a large play area will allow any youngsters in your party to burn off surplus energy, whilst their parents can simply relax in most pleasant surroundings.

A good range of food is available at the Old Ship Inn, including ploughman's, soups and salads, as well as chicken dishes, fish dishes, steaks and daily specials. To accompany your meal, real ales from both Courage and Wadworth are available, as well as farmhouse ciders and a good selection of wines. The food is well-presented and the portions quite ample, a perfect complement to this walk through the undulating countryside of the southern Cotswolds, where in a fold in the landscape we discover the source of one of the country's best known rivers. Telephone: 01666 840222.

- **HOW TO GET THERE:** Luckington lies on the B4040 road which runs between Malmesbury and the A46 at Old Sodbury. The Old Ship Inn fronts onto the main road in the centre of the village.
- **PARKING:** Opposite the Old Ship Inn is Luckington's village green. There is room for considerate roadside parking in the vicinity of this green.
- **LENGTH OF THE WALK:** 6 miles. Maps: OS Landranger 173 Swindon and Devizes and OS Explorer 168 Stroud, Tetbury and Malmesbury (GR 833840).

THE WALK

1. Walk across the village green in Luckington to the telephone box, before following the lane signposted to Sopworth that runs alongside the Old Ship Inn. In 300 yards, just past a side road named Northend, follow the footpath on the left up some steps. At the top of the steps, follow the footpath to the right into an open field by a stable block. Head across this field, bearing half left, to reach a stile in the middle of the opposite hedgerow. In the following field, head across – bearing slightly left – to a stile in the opposite hedgerow. In a third field, follow the left-hand field boundary to a gate in the top corner where the footpath joins a lane.

2. Follow this lane to the left, before it bears right in front of Wick Farm. Continue down this lane to Luckley Farm. Bear left just past the farmhouse and, in a few yards, descend the bank on the right to reach a handgate and an open field. Head across this field to a gate in the far top right corner, crossing a small stone footbridge along

81

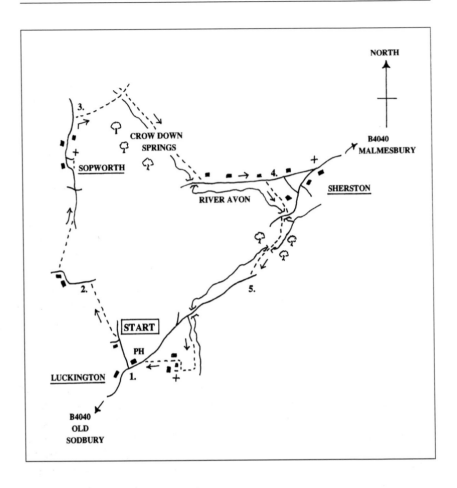

the way that crosses a normally dry stream bed. In the next field, cross diagonally to the far right corner to reach a gateway and a lane. Turn left and follow this lane for 500 yards into Sopworth. Where the lane bears left in the village, follow the footpath directly ahead for a short distance to reach the church. Turn left along Church Lane to rejoin the main road. Turn right, and continue out of the village.

3. About 350 yards out of the village, turn right along a track which drops down into a shallow valley containing what is usually the dry bed of the infant River Avon. Just up the hill past the river, turn right to follow a signposted footpath through a gateway. Follow this path along the right edges of the next four fields, passing Crow Down Springs that feed the Avon along the way. At the far side of the fourth field, pass through a gateway and bear half left across a final field towards a red-brick cottage. In the left corner of this field, by an electricity substation, pass through a gateway to join a lane. Turn left, and follow this lane towards Sherston for 1/2 mile.

4. Just past a property called Hillberry, cross a stone stile on the right to follow the footpath signposted to Brook Hill. Follow this path across the top of a field, the Avon down below in the valley. At the far side of the field, drop downhill to a handgate by the river and follow the path out to the B4040. Turn right, cross the Avon and then turn left over a stile to follow the footpath signposted to the Grove. Bear right in this meadow, and follow what is a tributary stream of the Avon upstream to a footbridge. Cross the river, before turning right to follow a riverside path through some trees. In 300 yards, cross a stile and continue ahead to a second stile and an open field. Walk across this field to the far top left corner and a stone stile. Cross the next field to a stile some 40 yards opposite, and join a quiet lane.

5. Turn right and follow this lane for 1/2 mile to a ford in Luckington. Cross the adjoining footbridge, and turn left to follow a lane along by some cottages. Beyond the last cottage, continue along a raised path above the river. Continue on past a large property on the right, before bearing right up towards Luckington church. On reaching the driveway leading into Luckington Court, turn right and follow another drive past a cottage, before turning left along an enclosed bridleway. Follow this occasionally muddy track for 300 yards back to the B4040, before turning left to return to the village green in Luckington and the Old Ship Inn.

PLACES OF INTEREST NEARBY
Westonbirt Arboretum is situated 5 miles north of Luckington and is open all year round. It is especially worth visiting in the spring when the rhododendrons and azaleas are in full bloom, and in the autumn when the leaves are changing colour. Telephone the Tourist Information Centre at Malmesbury on 01666 823748 for further information.

THE BY BROOK SOUTH OF CASTLE COMBE

Castle Combe must surely be one of Britain's best known villages. That row of stone cottages alongside the packhorse bridge over the By Brook has featured on any number of greetings cards, calendars and chocolate box lids. The By Brook, a tributary of the Bristol Avon, carves a route through steep-sided and wooded valleys, surely some of the finest landscape in the Southwolds.

Castle Combe

The By Brook is a picturesque stream running from deep in the Southern Cotswolds through to the River Avon at Bathford, a mile or two east of Bath. In just a few short miles, it passes through a veritable Who's Who of Cotswold villages, including Castle Combe, Ford, Slaughterford and Box. Along this stretch of the river, the valley bottom is narrow, and bordered with interlocking spurs of land on either side, land that is well-covered with deciduous woodland. Much of the valley bottom is flat grazing meadows, with little sign of cultivation, whilst the waters of the By Brook itself have over the centuries been harnessed for milling. It is truly a lonely, secluded landscape, despite its proximity to both Bath and Bristol.

Along this stretch of the river, the By Brook adds beauty and delight to Castle Combe, Ford and Long Dean. Castle Combe probably needs little introduction. Ever since it won the accord of 'the prettiest village in England' back in 1962, there has been no looking back as far as visitor numbers are concerned. From the packhorse bridge over the By Brook, the view extends up the main street past exquisite medieval domestic architecture as far as the Market Cross, the village church and the White Hart Inn. It is to the wool trade that Castle Combe owes its prosperity, with the Market Cross being the site of an annual sheep fair on St George's Day until the early years of the 20th century.

Ford loses some of its charm due to the presence of the busy A420 main road running between Bristol and Chippenham. There is a rather plain church alongside the main road, a fine pub down by the By Brook and a number of handsome stone properties, but in all truth it is a village that most visitors hurry past as they head along what was formerly the main road to London. Upstream of Ford is an altogether different settlement – Long Dean. This is a hamlet that the casual visitor would never stumble across, lying as it does down a narrow lane which is itself only accessible from a minor unclassified road. Here is a collection of cottages and former mills deep in the By Brook valley, very much a rural idyll.

After a delightfully secluded walk through the By Brook valley above Long Dean, the walk returns to Castle Combe. At the top of the main street, opposite the Market Cross, lies the White Hart Inn. The White Hart is not surprisingly constructed of the mellow local limestone, a traditional theme that is matched internally by flagstones, old beams and a fine open fireplace. With wooden tables, high-backed settles and cushioned window seats, this is the perfect place to relax. Around the bar are a number of prints, photographs and artefacts, including a horse harness and several old cider pots.

A tempting selection of bar meals is available at the White Hart, running from salads and sandwiches through to more substantial dishes that might typically include Cumberland sausages, a variety of steaks, chicken tikka and deep fried Brie. Being in Wiltshire, a glass of beer from the Wadworth brewery in Devizes comes highly recommended, possibly their flagship 6X brew, or their Farmer's Glory. If your taste is for something non-alcoholic, the White Hart has been known to produce cream teas, which in high summer could be enjoyed in the inn's secluded and shady rear courtyard. Telephone: 01249 782295.

- **HOW TO GET THERE/PARKING:** Halfway between Chippenham and Acton Turville, the B4039 passes through Upper Castle Combe. A well-signposted car park for visitors to Castle Combe lies alongside this B road.
- **LENGTH OF THE WALK:** 5½ miles. Maps: OS Landranger 173 Swindon and Devizes and OS Explorer 156 Chippenham and Bradford-on-Avon (GR 845777).

THE WALK

1. Leave the car park in Upper Castle Combe, turn right to reach a road junction and then right again to follow the lane downhill that leads to Castle Combe. Shortly, on a bend, bear right along a side turning that passes some cottages and the old village school. Where this lane bears right just past the school, cross a stile on the left and continue along the left edge of a field. Shortly, this path becomes enclosed and runs alongside the local golf course. When the path enters the golf course itself, keep to the wall on the left for a short distance before continuing downhill along a shady enclosed track. At the foot of the slope, turn right in front of a stile before continuing along an enclosed path, which drops downhill through woodland to rejoin the golf course. Follow the left edge of the golf course to a metalled road, follow this to the right and, at the next junction, turn left over a bridge to cross the By Brook. Continue along the road for 200 yards until, just past the tee for hole 4, fork left to follow the signposted footpath above Broadmead Brook. In 300 yards, keep on the path as it bears right to reach Nettleton Mill.

2. Turn left just past the first building, and continue following the footpath which borders Broadmead Brook, only now on the opposite bank. In 600 yards, cross a stile and follow a bridleway to the left over a clapper bridge. Continue along this track on uphill for ½ mile to a lane, turn left and follow this lane for ½ mile to a road junction.

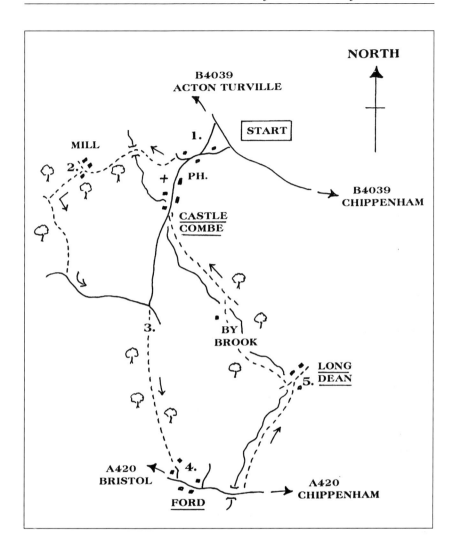

3. Cross the metal gate on the right alongside this junction, before turning left to follow a woodland path. In 300 yards, cross a stile and continue along the top left-hand edge of a field, with fine views across a tributary valley of the By Brook to the right. Towards the far side of this field, bear right by a marker post and head downhill to the bottom right corner of the field. Continue along a steep rough path down through a belt of trees and, in the next field, drop downhill to the valley bottom and cross a footbridge over a stream.

Walk the whole length of the valley bottom field ahead and, in the far right corner, bear right to join a woodland path. Follow this path through to a field, and continue ahead to a stile in the left corner. Continue along a lane – Park Lane – down to the A420 in Ford.

4. Turn left, and follow the A420 for 250 yards, keeping to the grass verge once the pavement ends at the left turn to Castle Combe. Cross the By Brook and, very soon, cross a stile on the left. Keep ahead across the meadow to a stile on the far side, before continuing ahead along a woodland path above the river to a gateway and another field. Keep ahead on the level to join the riverbank on the opposite side of the field, before continuing to another gateway and a footbridge across the river. Continue following the By Brook – now on the right – to another footbridge where the river is crossed once again. Continue ahead, the river is now on the left, to a stile in the far left corner of the field.

5. Cross this stile, and detour to the right if you wish to explore Long Dean. For the main walk, follow the track to the left across the By Brook before crossing a stile on the right into a meadow. Keep directly ahead, the river on the right, until you reach the riverbank below a sewage works. Follow the river upstream for 600 yards to an isolated cottage. Just past this cottage, cross a footbridge in the right corner of the field over the By Brook, before turning left along a rough valley bottom field. At the far end of this field, turn right uphill through some bushes to join a main track. Turn left, and follow this track for ½ mile, well above the By Brook. Cross a stile in the far left corner of a final field, before continuing along an enclosed path by the river to a bridge and the lane leading into Castle Combe. Turn right, follow the road through the village – passing the White Hart Inn by the Market Cross – before continuing uphill for 400 yards back to the car park.

PLACES OF INTEREST NEARBY

The town of Corsham lies just 6 miles south of Castle Combe. *Corsham Court*, whose Georgian state rooms contain Flemish paintings and fine English furniture, is open to the public on a regular basis. Telephone: 01249 701610.

WALK 19

THE BY BROOK AT BOX

The By Brook to the east of Bath flows through an appealing landscape of rolling hillsides and deep valleys, interspersed with villages and hamlets hewn of the local stone. This varied short walk takes you up to Box Hill, with splendid views along the way, and then down to the riverside meadows for a leisurely stroll back to Box village.

The By Brook at Box

The village of Box experienced something of a boom during the 18th century, not dissimilar to an American gold rush. The hillsides that overshadow the village contain their own gold – golden limestone – which was in great demand at the time for the construction of those magnificent terraced streets in nearby Bath. Legend maintains that the stone was originally discovered many years earlier by St Aldhelm, with this the most famous stone of the Great Oolite formation being named 'St Aldhelm Box Stone'. The Box stone mines penetrated deep under these hillsides, employing hundreds of local men who carved an intricate network of tunnels and passageways beneath Box Hill.

Perhaps the most famous tunnel in Box, however, has nothing to do with the stone mines. Brunel's Great Western Railway ran through the village, and Box Hill provided quite an obstacle for the line's engineers. In the end, one of the most impressive railway tunnels in Britain was carved through the hillside. Nearly two miles in length, Box Tunnel took four years to complete. The early part of this walk passes through Box with its viewpoint overlooking the western entrance to the tunnel, before climbing steeply up Quarry Hill to reach Box Hill. The views are quite magnificent, extending across the valley to Colerne on the opposite side. Box Hill itself is a maze of side lanes and tracks, along which isolated ranks of cottages and houses lie dotted in a completely random and unplanned manner.

A steep descent down hillside lanes brings the walk to Drewett's Mill and the By Brook, with the riverbank being our constant companion all of the way back into Box. In this section of its course, the river meanders slowly across flat meadowland, with willow, hawthorn and bramble forming the riverside habitat. As well as swan, moorhen and coot, sharp eyes may pick out the occasional kingfisher or dipper along this stretch of the river. Watermills were common along the By Brook, Drewett's Mill being originally an overshot wheel with a 10 foot diameter, which drove three pairs of stones. Today, many of these mills have been converted into attractive residences or transformed to house other business activities. Box Mill, at the end of the walk, now houses Peter Gabriel's Real World Music recording studios, attracting world famous recording artistes to this quiet corner of Wiltshire.

High on Box Hill lies the Quarryman's Arms. Quite naturally constructed of the local limestone, the inn presents a rather diminutive appearance from the road. It has been likened to a single-storey Victorian railway station, although the nearest railway tracks pass hundreds of feet below the hillside deep in Box Tunnel. This would have been the watering hole for thirsty stone miners, and this era lives on in the prints, mine plans and mining memorabilia that adorn the walls of this hostelry.

The cosy interior of the Quarryman's Arms has a picture window with quite exceptional views across the valley. The food available at the inn ranges from familiar options such as ploughman's, bangers and mash, steak and kidney pie and fish and chips, through to more unusual offerings such as Stilton and asparagus pancakes, steamed bass with mustard and tarragon sauce and warm salad of chicken and bacon. There are fine real ales, that might include Butcombe Bitter, Wadworth 6X and Wickwar Brand Oak Bitter. It may be a short walk – and the Quarryman's Arms may appear very early on along the route – but it is an opportune spot to rest awhile before dropping downhill to the By Brook. Telephone: 01225 743569.

- **HOW TO GET THERE:** Box lies 6 miles east of Bath on the main A4 Chippenham road.
- **PARKING:** The A365 joins the A4 at a set of traffic lights in the centre of Box. About 200 yards along the A4 in the Chippenham direction, a car park is signposted. Follow the signs down to the car park in the Market Place in Box.
- **LENGTH OF THE WALK:** 2½ miles. Maps: OS Landranger 173 Swindon and Devizes and OS Explorer 156 Chippenham and Bradford-on-Avon (GR 827686).

THE WALK

1. Leave the car park, turn right and follow the road back up to the A4. Turn right, and follow the main road up to the Box Tunnel viewpoint. Continue along the A4 for another 100 yards, before crossing a stile on the right, the path signposted to Quarry Hill. Walk directly uphill, before crossing a stile on the right which lies above the portals of the railway tunnel. In the next field, turn left and head uphill to a stile in the top field boundary, 40 yards down from the top left-hand corner. Cross the stile, turn left and follow Quarry Hill to a road junction on the hilltop.

2. Turn left, and follow the lane along past the local common and on to the Quarryman's Arms. Continue along the lane past the pub and, shortly, turn left downhill along Barnetts Hill. At the bottom of the hill, at a junction, cross into Hedgesparrow Lane and continue downhill to the busy A4.

3. Cross the A4, and follow the lane opposite down to Drewett's Mill and the By Brook. Turn left at the junction just past the river. In 30 yards, cross a stile in the hedge on the left, before following the left edge of a field down to a second stile. In the next field, bear right

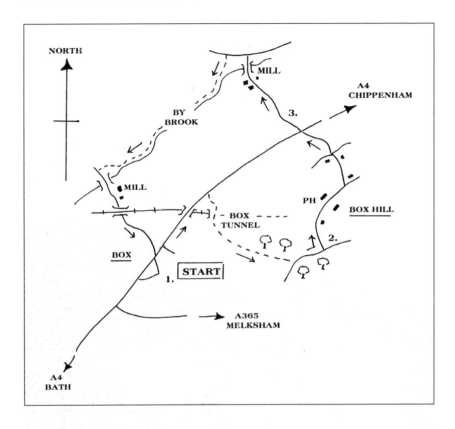

down to the By Brook. Follow the riverbank downstream for ³/₄ mile across the meadows. At the far side of the final field, cross a stile alongside the river and turn right to follow an enclosed path which runs above a stream on the left. Follow this path around to Mill Lane, just by the Real World recording studios. Follow Mill Lane up to the A4, before continuing down the lane opposite, signposted to the Market Place. This lane returns you to the car park.

PLACES OF INTEREST NEARBY

At Corsham, 4 miles from Box, visitors can be taken on guided tours of the *Underground Quarry*. This former stone mine is now a popular tourist attraction, which is signposted from the A4 as you approach Corsham. Telephone 01249 716288 for details of opening hours.

WALK 20
THE KENNET AND AVON CANAL NEAR BATH

Discover the finest natural landscape along the whole length of the Kennet and Avon Canal. Steep, wooded slopes come tumbling down the slopes of the Avon Valley, providing a spectacular backdrop to this exhilarating walk.

Narrowboats on the Kennet & Avon

A recent addition to the Cotswold Area of Outstanding Natural Beauty was the Avon Valley, extending south from Bath to Bradford-on-Avon. Sweeping hillsides, grazing meadows, clear rivers and cottages fashioned out of that delightful golden limestone produce a scene that would not be out of place any where in the 'wolds.

The walk begins at Bathampton, from where our steps climb the wooded slopes of the Brown's Folly Nature Reserve, before a steep descent into the heart of the Avon Valley. A pleasant riverside path is followed upstream to Dundas Aqueduct and the Kennet and Avon Canal.

Along the 3-mile section of canal followed on this walk, our steps also pass Dundas Wharf, Claverton Pumping Station and Hampton Wharf. Dundas Wharf marks the junction of the Kennet and Avon with the Somerset Coal Canal, whose first $1/4$ mile has been restored as moorings for narrow boats and pleasure craft. It is possible to walk this short section of the Somerset Coal Canal to reach a recently opened visitors centre and café.

Back in Bathampton, the canalside George Inn is one of the most popular watering holes in the Bath area. This attractive creeper-covered building consists of a collection of low-ceilinged rooms, with much exposed stonework and beams. Horse brasses, old rifles, oil paintings and sherry barrels add to the historical feel of the pub, where legend maintains that an underground passage leads off to the neighbouring church.

The menu at the George should appeal to all tastes. From ploughman's, salads and sandwiches through to vegetarian dishes and daily specials, there is certainly no shortage of choice. To accompany your meal, a glass of Courage Best or Directors would go down well, or perhaps a pint of Bass or Irish Beamish. Telephone: 01225 425079.

- **HOW TO GET THERE:** Approach from the A36 between Bath and Warminster. Less than 2 miles from the city centre, an unclassified road running north-east – Bathampton Lane – leads down to Bathampton village. Follow this road through the village, cross the Kennet and Avon Canal, and turn right into Tyning Lane.
- **PARKING:** Park on the roadside in the vicinity of Bathampton Primary School.
- **LENGTH OF THE WALK:** 7 miles. Maps: OS Landranger 172 Bristol and Bath and OS Explorer 155 Bristol and Bath (GR 778665).

THE WALK

1. Follow Tyning Lane from the main road for $1/4$ mile to reach the Bristol to Southampton railway line. Cross the railway before entering open fields. Head across to the pylon on the far side of the second field, just below a railway embankment, crossing one stile along the way. Cross the stile alongside this pylon, and follow the path up the railway embankment, across the River Avon and down to the busy A363. Follow the main road to the right, crossing the By Brook – a tributary of the Avon – before turning left off the

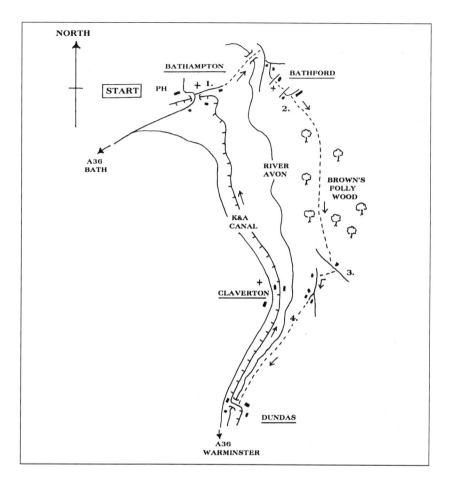

main road into Bathford. Almost immediately, turn right to follow Ostlings Lane uphill alongside the Crown Inn. On reaching Church Street, cross over and follow the tarmac path that runs to the left of St Swithun's church up to Pump Lane. Turn right, then left into an estate road called Mountain Wood. Where the road bears left into the estate, keep right on the grassy area up to a stile.

2. Cross this stile, and climb the hillside field ahead to the far top left corner. Cross a stile at this point to enter Brown's Folly Wood. Follow the main path uphill, and shortly, where the path divides into two parallel paths, keep to the right-hand lower route. Continue uphill for 150 yards to a prominent junction, and turn right. Ignore a

95

left turn in just 15 yards, and continue following the main woodland path. This climbs uphill for 600 yards to a junction on the hilltop almost on the edge of the woodland. Keep right and follow the woodland path along the edge of Brown's Folly Wood, an old wall in the undergrowth on the left. This path eventually descends the hillside to reach the A363 in ³/₄ mile. Follow the main road to the left for 50 yards to reach a driveway leading to a cottage.

3. Follow the path immediately to the right of this driveway down to a junction, and turn right to pass underneath a bridge carrying the main road. Several paths head off ahead. Take the path directly ahead, beyond an old stone slab stile, and continue downhill through the woodland to a stile. Continue along the well-worn path beyond this stile down to a stile in the corner of the field and the lane leading from Conkwell to Bathford. Follow this lane to the left for 300 yards before forking right along the access lane into Sheephouse Farm. Walk to the far end of the farmyard, before taking the enclosed permissive path on the right downhill into the valley. At the end of this path, cross a stile and follow the left edge of the next field downhill for 15 yards to a stile on the left. Cross this stile, and continue downhill through scrubland to reach a footbridge, a stile and the River Avon.

4. Follow the river upstream across four fields – in summer, incidentally, the river may well be out of sight behind long meadow grass. At the far side of the fourth field, cross a stile to the left of the Monkton Combe School Rowing Club, before climbing a flight of steps to reach the Kennet and Avon Canal. Turn right, cross Dundas Aqueduct, and follow the canal towpath to the right past a footbridge. Follow the towpath for 3 miles through the Avon Valley back to Bathampton, where you emerge alongside the primary school. Just 50 yards ahead is the George Inn.

PLACES OF INTEREST NEARBY
The centre of Bath lies just 2 miles from the end of the walk. Amongst the major attractions in Bath are the *Roman Baths, Bath Abbey*, and the *Royal Crescent*. Contact the Tourist Information Centre on 01225 477101. Alternatively, 2 miles south of Bathampton, on the hill above the A36, is the *American Museum* housed in what was formerly Claverton Manor. Telephone 01225 460503.